To

Low,

D0854783

# THE HANDBOOK OF
# FOREIGN BIRDS

## VOLUME TWO

# THE HANDBOOK OF
# FOREIGN BIRDS
## IN COLOUR
## VOLUME TWO

Their Care in Cage and Aviary

By A. RUTGERS

English Edition
edited by K. A. Norris

BLANDFORD PRESS

LONDON

From material in
*Tropische Volière Vogels*
by A. Rutgers, published by
Littera Scripta Manet, Joppe, Holland.
(Copyright—all rights reserved.)

Colour printed in photogravure by D. H. Greaves Ltd., Scarborough
Text printed and books bound
in Great Britain by Richard Clay (The Chaucer Press) Ltd.,
Bungay, Suffolk

# CONTENTS

# ACKNOWLEDGMENTS

Most of the colour photographs were taken by Mr Jeremy McCabe by arrangement with The Zoological Gardens, Regent's Park, London; Chessington Zoo, Surrey; Whipsnade Zoological Park, Beds.; Mr Mark Harris, Sydenham (owner of the lovebirds).

Acknowledgment is due to Mrs Philippa Scott for her photographs of waterfowl, Nos. 34, 36–43; to Harry Y. Lacey, Industrial Colour Slide Services, Chippenham, Wilts. for Nos. 64, 115–118; to Barnaby's Picture Library for Nos. 23 and 24; to Mr Horst Müller-Schmidz for No. 119.

A special acknowledgment is made to Mr K. A. Norris who edited this book for the English reader and wrote additional descriptions.

# INTRODUCTION

The general principles of foreign bird keeping have been very fully discussed in the first volume of this work and detailed instructions have been given for the design, construction and furnishing of aviaries and for the feeding and breeding of the smaller species. It now remains to consider the special requirements of the parrots and parrot-like species which are great favourites with many fanciers, and also the doves, quail, pheasants and waterfowl which form separate and highly specialized groups.

With a few exceptions the species in each of these groups are suitable only as inhabitants of large aviaries which must be adapted to their special needs.

Although Budgerigars have now become domesticated and consequently can no longer be included under the general heading of 'foreign birds' they are nevertheless members of the parrot family and are by far the most widely kept cage bird in England today, exceeding in popularity even the canary and the larger parrots. Many fanciers still like to keep a few of these birds in conjunction with a collection of foreigners and although they have an exhaustive literature of their own it has been considered desirable to include in this volume chapters on their maintenance and breeding, with particular reference to the principles of colour production.

Colour mutations occur in most species from time to time although they seldom survive to reproduce their kind in a wild state. In the hands of an experienced breeder however they may be used not only to perpetuate their own abnormal colouring but their offspring may in turn be used to produce yet other colour variations. Colour breeding is a fascinating branch of the hobby and the laws governing mutations and the influence of hormones on colour production are discussed in some detail.

The bird fancier has a unique opportunity to study the breeding behaviour of his birds at close quarters, and to obtain information of considerable scientific value which is not readily obtainable from observation of birds in a wild state. A notebook should therefore always be available and full details of mating displays and nesting operations recorded. From time to time the information thus collected should be published in journals devoted to aviculture and ornithology as it may well prove to be invaluable to other and less experienced fanciers and also to scientific workers.

It has occasionally been necessary to refer to the first volume in order to avoid repetition. Unfortunately the scientific nomenclature is still under constant revision, and some of the names used may not be familiar to readers, while the English names are sometimes apt to convey an erroneous impression of the bird. In both Latin and English therefore synonyms are given where it is considered that these may prove of assistance in identifying a species.

It is hoped that the book will give further pleasure to those interested in this fascinating and all-absorbing hobby.

# 1   FOODS

*Quail, Doves, Pigeons*

The small doves and quail require a seed mixture containing: 25% canary seed; 25% large white millet or yellow millet; 25% senegal millet and 10% hemp, to which may be added 15% groats or 5% groats and 10% dari.

For the larger species, whole or broken wheat, red and white dari and buckwheat in equal proportions should be added to the above mixture.

All quail are partly insectivorous and in addition to the seed mixture, some live food such as mealworms, beetles, gentles and ant cocoons must be provided. Grated raw or boiled meat may be offered occasionally as a change. Some of the doves will also take a little live food from time to time.

Green food, weed seeds and grated raw carrot are also beneficial and as these birds do not shell the seed they must always have access to a supply of good sharp grit, to aid in grinding and digesting their food.

Some species of pigeons live almost exclusively on fruit, and suitable diets for these are mentioned when describing the individual species.

## *Waterfowl*

Wheat, coarse bran, maize meal and fish meal form the main ingredients of a good duck feed, in the proportion of 55%, 15% and 15%. Some fanciers add stale bread and scraps from the table. This mixture should be given well-moistened as ducks cannot pick up and eat dry food.

If the birds are fed in the open, the wheat may be given separately, in a trough of water, which will prevent sparrows from stealing it. It is a great advantage if ducks can have access to meadowland where they will spend much time foraging for slugs, snails, worms and insects of all kinds and will eat quantities of fresh, tender grass.

For those who prefer to buy ready-mixed foods, there are good proprietary duck meals which provide a complete and well-balanced diet which can be obtained from most corn merchants.

## *Parrots and Parrakeets*

With the exception of the Brush-tongued Parrots, which include the Lories and Lorikeets, all members of the parrot family feed largely on seeds and suitable mixtures are supplied by most seed merchants.

The basis of all mixtures should be good quality white millet and bold canary seed and most Budgerigar breeders now use these seeds only. Some prefer to include yellow and senegal millet and a suitable mixture for these very popular little parrakeets can be made up as follows:

$\frac{1}{4}$ part each of bold canary seed, white, yellow and senegal millet.

As a change, the proportion of senegal millet may be halved and the balance replaced with groats but the latter is a very fattening food and should not be given too often.

For the larger parrakeets the following mixture is suitable:

$\frac{1}{4}$ canary seed, $\frac{1}{4}$ mixed white and yellow millet, and $\frac{1}{8}$ each of groats, sunflower, hemp and fresh peanuts.

Although most species can be kept alive and in good condition on these mixtures for many years, it will be found that it is the 'little extra' which makes all the difference. Never fail therefore to provide variety and to consider the special requirements of individual birds.

Buckwheat, whole oats, barley, wheat and maize may all be used occasionally to make variety in the mixture supplied to the larger species and all enjoy millet sprays. In addition, fresh green food such as chickweed, dandelion, lettuce and spinach should always be available and raw carrot, sweet apple and other sound fruit may be offered.

As mentioned elsewhere, the birds should always have a supply of fresh twigs and branches from which they can strip the buds and bark and for this purpose all forms of fruit trees, prunus and hawthorn are most suitable. Never use laurel or laburnum, both of which are very poisonous.

It will be found that the consumption of green food and fruit will greatly increase when the birds are feeding their young, and at this time it is advisable also to offer a little bread and milk made with stale brown bread and fresh milk sweetened with sugar or honey. Care must be taken however to ensure that it is never left before the birds when it has become tainted or sour.

Some species also consume a quantity of insects and a few mealworms may be offered daily and also fresh ant cocoons when available. A clean, sharp grit with minerals, charcoal and cuttlefish bone should always be provided as essential to the preservation of health.

One word of warning: the pet parrot should not be given all kinds of scraps from the table. As titbits, sweet biscuits or small pieces of plain cake may be offered occasionally, but parrots should not have butter or other forms of fat or any kind of meat as these they cannot tolerate and their health will soon suffer.

Should it be desired to hand-rear young parrots or parrakeets, the following mixture may be used:

Rusks, crushed and moistened with sufficient water to make the crumbs soft but not pappy, with an equal quantity of finely ground millet and canary seed from which the husks have been blown away, and with a few drops of cod liver oil or vitamin C and D in liquid form added.

Suitable foods for the Lories and Lorikeets are mentioned in the text dealing specially with these birds. The foods for Pheasants and Partridges are given on pages 17–18. References to special feeding are given under the descriptions of individual species.

## 2   PHEASANT KEEPING

Pheasants are not suitable for keeping indoors and should only be included in a fancier's collection if plenty of out-door accommodation is available, preferably some corner of an orchard or woodland. In country districts many pheasants can be seen. In addition to well known species such as the Reeves's, Silver, Golden, Lady Amherst, and the common pheasants, there are to be found in fanciers' collections pheasants which until recently were considered rare and expensive, including the Blue Eared, Swinhoe's, Scintillating Copper, Elliot's and many others.

Flights of 6 ft or over are advisable and may be used for a mixed collection of pheasants and perching birds, such as doves, parrakeets or small finches.

It is largely due to the fact that pheasants can be safely associated with other species that fanciers are encouraged to keep them. Since they spend most of the time on the ground they seldom interfere with perching birds which usually seek out the highest available perches. Naturally the latter will descend to the ground occasionally during the day to scratch around the feeding, drinking and bathing dishes and to hunt for insects and other foodstuffs in the soil, but at other times most remain high above the ground. Life in the aviary is therefore made more interesting and varied by the addition of a pair of quail, pheasants or colourful small ducks.

Even in a well-planted flight, populated by small finches, a trio of Golden Pheasants or Lady Amherst Pheasants could be included without interference with breeding operations. The large Silver Pheasants and the Blue Eared Pheasants are better kept in the company of a few of the larger parrakeets. On several occasions I have missed some Zebra Finch fledglings and other young foreign finches, which had just tried their wings, and have discovered that they had been eaten by the Silver Pheasants. Ordinary Budgerigars are quite able to look after themselves and are safe in the flight with the pheasants.

Most pheasants are polygamous, and two or three hens can usually run with one cock. The common pheasant will take as many as seven wives, and the eggs will still all be fertile in the spring. Some species, however, are monogamous, as for instance the Scintillating Copper Pheasant, and the Peacock Pheasant, both of which will accept one hen only.

Books have been written especially for the pheasant fancier; here we shall discuss only some of the more popular species and give general directions for housing, care and breeding.

Although an ordinary flight of at least 12 ft by 18 ft would comfortably house a few pheasants together with other birds, it would be more advisable – provided always that room and the necessary funds are available – to have special aviaries for the pheasants. These should be at least 30 ft to 45 ft long and have a width of 10–12 ft with a height of 8 ft. Most of the species of pheasants we describe here are quite hardy and the shelters need not be fitted with doors. The windows must, however, be kept closed, otherwise the continuous draught might well cause the death of all the birds.

If pheasant keeping is seriously contemplated, then the beginning should not be on too small a scale. For instance, at least four runs should be made next to each other and built so that the range can be extended at any time if so desired. In most cases additions will eventually be required as the collection grows and new species are acquired. (Fig. 1)

The sectional drawing of the shelter shows very clearly that a passage runs behind it, from which food and drink can be supplied. This passage needs to be divided from the shelters only by wire-covered frame partitions.

The roof should slope down towards the back. Care should be taken to see that the back is not directly on the boundary of one's property; otherwise neighbours may complain. The roof should be covered with adequate rain-proofing material. The shelters can be made of wood and are best set on concrete flooring. It is unnecessary to go into further details about the outside flights. If other birds are

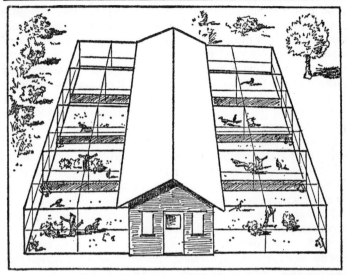

FIG 1 *Aviary for pheasants with night accommodation. The range can readily be extended to provide for additional pairs as required. The divisions are of small gauge wire netting but should be close boarded to a height of 18 to 24 in. from the ground to prevent birds in adjoining aviaries from fighting through the wire. There is a passage at the rear of the night quarters from which food and water can be supplied without disturbing the birds by entering the aviaries.*

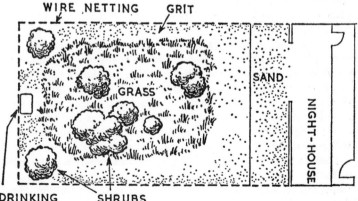

to be kept in conjunction with the pheasants, then their size must be proportionately larger. The partitions between the various runs should be made of the smallest mesh wire on account of the fighting habits of the cocks and to obviate this as much as possible the partitions should be of boarding or covered with rush matting for a height of 2 ft from the ground, or a brick or concrete wall constructed of similar height. Such a wall could, with advantage, be built all round the outer perimiter of the four runs. The pheasants would then have much more seclusion.

If roosting perches are provided in the flights – preferably thick ones – the pheasants will always be found sleeping outside at night.

If it is desired to ensure that the birds roost under cover, perches should only be placed in the shelter, otherwise they will almost always choose those which are in the open, even in frost and snow and will not roost under shelter unless compelled to do so by lack of perches elsewhere. They should be arranged in such a way that the birds cannot damage their long tails when roosting or flying. The distance from the back wall should be at least 4 ft 6 in., but they need not be higher than 3 ft–4 ft from the ground.

Communicating doors should be made between the aviaries. The wire netting should be buried into the soil all round the outside of the aviaries to a depth of at least 20 in. to guard against mice and other intruders. If small perching birds are also to be kept in the aviaries, and enclosed shelters are provided, an entrance for use by the pheasants should be made at ground level and another, high up, for the smaller birds.

Special attention must be given to the ground of the aviary. If a good porous sandy soil is not available, ample drainage must be provided by artificial means. The soil should be dug out to a depth of 3 ft and a layer of rubble or ashes put in. A layer of gravel should be placed over this, and there should be a final covering of good soil, mixed with peat and sharp sand. Under the shelter roof at the rear of the aviary there should be a 4 in. layer of sharp sand, where it will not get wet, as pheasants are very partial to sand baths.

Pheasants have a habit of walking round and round the boundaries of their enclosures and it is as well to provide them with a dry path, which can be of gravel or concrete on which coarse gravel should be scattered while the cement is still wet. This will give a roughened surface and look more artistic. This path will prevent the ground from becoming a mud bath during wet weather. The corners of the aviary should, if possible, be rounded and all angles eliminated as the pheasants' long tails are easily damaged when the birds continually pace round and round the boundary. As an alternative precaution, some shrubs or small pine trees can be planted in the corners quite close to the wire netting. Elder trees and rhododendrons lend themselves well for this purpose. Yews should be avoided, as the foliage is very poisonous.

There are many ways in which an aviary can be made more attractive. A narrow ornamental pond can be constructed to run through all four flights with reeds or bamboo planted along the borders. Small bridges or old tree trunks will beautify the interior. Parrots should not be kept in an aviary thus ornamented as they will quickly destroy all plants but many birds, such as the insect-eaters, do little damage. Turf is greatly appreciated as flooring by all birds, both large and small.

A thick layer of hay or straw may be placed in the shelter during spells of severe weather; this also will be appreciated by the pheasants and if the perches are then removed so that they are compelled to remain on the bed of straw at night, frost-bitten legs will be avoided. The straw also keeps their stomachs warm when they are sleeping at night. If the floor of the shelter is made of cement or concrete, it should be covered with a layer of peat or sharp sand during the summer.

Nylon or perlon netting, quite a new material, is now being used as a top covering for pheasant aviaries and is a most successful means of preventing the birds from damaging their heads when they fly upwards, as they are always apt to do if frightened. This material has been in use too short a time to test its durability but good results are expected. If this material is used it must be so fixed that it is quite flexible, with plenty of 'give'.

The inside of the shelter should be lime-washed. It is advisable to cover part of the flight with plexiglass or double plastic sheeting, extending 4–5 ft from the shelter. On rainy days this will permit the birds to be in the open without being exposed to the rain.

Most species of pheasants are accustomed to cold and, in fact, seem to like it; therefore they must not be exposed to excessive heat of the sun. If the aviary is situated amongst trees or in an orchard, useful shade will be provided, otherwise dense growing shrubs should be planted in the flights to give the birds the necessary protection from the sun. Rhododendrons are very suitable for this purpose.

During the mating season the cocks are apt to persecute the hens and the latter must be able to find some retreat otherwise they will soon become exhausted and may then be badly scalped. The shrubs will afford them some protection, but in some cases it may be necessary to remove the cock for a while to give the hens a little peace. Bad tempered cocks are best kept in a separate pen and only allowed to run with the hens for a short time for mating.

## 3   THE ACQUISITION OF PHEASANTS

When obtaining stock the birds should always be bought from a breeder of repute in whom the purchaser can have complete confidence. If trios are offered, a guarantee should be obtained that the birds are not related. Nothing is so deleterious to pheasants as close inbreeding, especially as the strains available are none too pure in the best of circumstances.

The purity of Golden and Lady Amherst Pheasants in particular is often in doubt due to the fact that these two species have so frequently been interbred in the past, resulting in a strain of Amhersts showing red and orange flecking on the breast and yellow legs. It is difficult especially to gauge the purity of the young birds; it may be necessary to wait until they assume their full colour, and that only happens in the summer of their second year.

It is, however, advisable to obtain young birds; these are best for breeding and are more easily mated. The cock and hens should be bought from different breeders; the birds are then less likely to be related. It is sometimes difficult to tell the age of adult birds. Although they remain fertile for 12–15 years, their purchase may lead to disappointments as unscrupulous breeders will usually

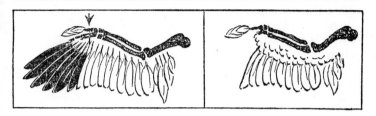

FIG 2 *Wing of a pheasant, left—before, and right, after pinioning*

*If pheasants or ducks are to be kept at liberty in a garden or paddock it is usually necessary to restrict their powers of flight to prevent them straying and this may be effected by clipping the flight feathers of one wing. This however is a temporary measure only as the birds will recover their full flight following each moult. If the flight is to be permanently restricted, a portion of the wing carrying the outer six primaries must be amputated immediately forward of the bastard wing or 'thumb' as indicated by an arrow on the left hand drawing. This operation may be carried out on newly hatched chicks or ducklings by simply snipping off the tip of one wing with sharp scissors. At this early age the operation will cause no pain or bleeding as the bone is still soft but with adult birds the amputation requires considerable skill and experience and is best performed by a veterinary surgeon.*

attempt to dispose of old birds when they are approaching the end of their 'breeding life'.

Correct management is most important if it is desired to have quiet and confident birds. If they are spoken to quietly on arrival before they are placed in the aviary, wild flying which may result in damaged heads, will often be prevented. The birds should be left to their own resources for some time and disturbed as little as possible. Drinking water and grain should, of course, be available, and also green food. They will soon settle down. They can be left together all winter; young birds get accustomed to one another easily and mating will probably run a normal course and the eggs will be fertile.

Naturally, it is essential that in the first place the food is varied and of excellent quality; this may well determine the fertility of the eggs and the vitality of the chicks. Good proprietary pheasant foods are obtainable, both seed mixtures and also pellets. Root crops and potatoes are also eaten. During the early months of the year the pheasants need extra oats and hemp seed and during the coldest months extra maize. All kinds of green food should be provided – grass, chickweed, lettuce, scotch kale, and such like.

Meatmeal must be mixed with the food. Oyster grit is indispensable and old mortar rubble is excellent. Finely chopped raw meat, insects of all kinds and earthworms are eaten greedily but it is preferable that the birds should not be allowed to eat the latter as pheasants are very subject to a disease known as gapes which is caused by parasitic roundworms, usually *Syngamus trachea*, of which earthworms are the host. Pheasants are omniverous and, as with all birds, a varied diet is most beneficial. It is, however, important to watch that the birds do not eat too much, for it is ruinous to the prospects of a successful breeding season if either the cocks or hens are over-fat. The grain feed can be omitted now and again in the evenings – one handful suffices for two birds – and every bird should have at most only one handful of pellets. It will be found that they eat considerably less than domestic fowls or tame ducks.

Mealworms, the ideal extra rearing food for the young birds, are a treat and will be useful for taming the adults for they will soon learn readily to approach to take these from the hand. Naturally every fancier is anxious that his birds should become tame and confiding.

An adequate supply of fresh drinking water should always be available and fountains or troughs of a design which can readily be kept clean should always be used. The water will remain fresh much longer if the containers are so placed that they are always in the shade. Baths are not necessary as pheasants indulge only in dust-bathing.

# 4 BREEDING OF PHEASANTS

With most species of pheasants laying begins towards the end of April and sometime continues until the end of July. Various methods of hatching and rearing can be adopted. Some species hatch and rear their own young very well as, for instance, the Golden and the Lady Amherst. The use of bantams, especially Wyandottes, Silkies and Bankiva hens, as foster parents is universal and the results are usually excellent. The first batch of eggs especially may be hatched by bantams; the last batch may be left to the pheasant hen herself to hatch and rear.

The hatching period varies somewhat; the Golden Pheasant takes 23 days, the Lady Amherst Pheasant 24 days. If a pheasant hen be left to hatch her own eggs, other hens should be removed to another run, as also should the cock, if he tries to disturb the sitting hen.

When a bantam hen is used, she should be set by herself with 10 eggs in a box without an artificial floor. A hollow should be made in the sand, and lined with hay, sprinkled with insect powder and the eggs placed in this artificial nest. The bantam should not have feathered legs as the feathers are apt to get under the eggs or small chicks and lift them from the nest when she moves. If she leaves the nest regularly to eat and perform her natural functions and returns without undue delay, all should be well. The run should be covered with sand and some sieved ashes; then she can take her daily dust-bath. As an alternative to the hay nest, it may be beneficial to lay the eggs on an upturned and hollowed turf as this will help to maintain the correct degree of moisture.

Hatching in an incubator is quite a different matter. There are on the market efficient and inexpensive machines in which 50–60 eggs can be hatched in one batch. Many quail, partridges and pheasants are born annually in incubators. Several points require special attention; the chief is maintaining the right degree of moisture (58%) and a temperature of 103 °F (39 °C). A great deal depends on the care of the eggs; they should be turned twice a day and aired daily from the third to the nineteenth day. This applies to pheasants' eggs in particular.

The eggs should preferably be set in the machine with the thick end upwards. After about a fortnight the embryo chick will turn itself lengthways with its head to the highest point, therefore to the air chamber.

It is advisable to place eggs of even size in the incubator. Even if the eggs have been incubated by a bantam hen, it may be just as well to take them away from her the day before they are due to hatch and set them in the incubator, as some bantams are apt to lead the first two or three chicks to hatch away from the nest and the remaining eggs then become chilled before the young birds can emerge. The young can be returned to the hen the day after they have left the egg.

After the chicks have appeared extra care is necessary for a time. The bantam should have an enclosed run, moved onto fresh grass

FIG 3 *Rearing pen for pheasant chicks or ducklings. The run is divided by wire netting with an opening of a size suitable to allow the young birds to pass through but not the brooding hen. Feeding can be done in the outer run which prevents the hen from depriving the chicks of food. They will easily find their way back to the hen for warmth when necessary. The run is movable and can be transferred to fresh ground daily. When raining the top can be covered with felt or transparent sheeting.*

daily and entirely covered by plastic during bad weather. Pheasants cannot stand damp. It is still better to have a run of two compartments divided by a slide door and with one compartment permanently covered with some waterproof material which nevertheless admits full light. During wet weather the chicks may then be confined to the covered compartment and on fine days allowed the freedom of the whole run.

If the young have been hatched in an incubator and no bantams are available to act as foster mothers, a brooder will be needed. The young must remain inside for the first few weeks, and can then go into an open run during the day, in fine sunny weather.

A good quality commercial pheasant or turkey rearing food should be used, with ants' eggs, mealworms, bread and milk, canary seed, canary rearing food and finely ground raw oxheart added. Pellets in which everything necessary has been incorporated are the easiest to use, with ants' eggs and mealworms added. Charcoal and fine grit should not be forgotten. A little mild antiseptic should be added every third day to the drinking water to prevent intestinal disturbances. Many suitable preparations are available. With a little care rearing under the foster-mother presents little difficulty. After a few days finely chopped chickweed and lettuce should be added to the rearing food. Pheasants take to green food gradually. If the young pheasants run about freely with the bantam, their wings must be clipped or they will start to roost too high up in the trees at an early age and may be completely lost. When they reach the stage of wanting to roost on their own they must be caught and put in the aviary.

## 5   THE KEEPING OF ORNAMENTAL WATERFOWL

A whole book could be written on this subject, but I intend to refer only to the well-known species which I have kept in my own flights for many years.

A pond will be the first essential for this special hobby; it is soon dug and should be on a very small scale. One or two pairs of ducks can easily be kept on a small area of land; the cost of constructing the pond and of the necessary wire fencing need not be ruinous. Neither is the price of a pair of ornamental ducks excessive, and in any case a beginning can be made with the less expensive species.

If land alongside a brook is available, or if there is a natural tarn or fen, the possibilities are endless. Large numbers of ducks can then be kept for they obtain their food mostly from the water, so that their keep costs little. The collection can consist of many species, even swans and geese.

The borders of the pond can be left to grow naturally, but care must be taken to keep down natural enemies such as rats and other vermin. Many a paradise for fish and ducks has been created on small areas of private property although it may take four to eight years to become established. More and more plants, brought from far and near by birds visiting these newly-created ponds, will add to the

Fig 4 *Large pond with natural island and surroundings.*

existing flora. Birds can be watched all the year round. During migration time many wild ducks also arrive. Breeding baskets can be placed close to the water during spring while a floating feeding-table may be made, and can be supported by a couple of empty oil drums, and moored to the bank by a chain. The illustration shows such a feeding island; all around the pond thick shrubbery has shot up, hiding the pond from view and giving the 'wild' guests a sense of security.

If a brook or river runs along or through the property quite different opportunities are offered. Adjoining the border a fenced off pool can be constructed and fed from the stream. In this the ducks can be kept. Wide ditches, with no current, may have duck ponds made in the same way. By renewing the water regularly, very good accommodation for ducks can be provided. A number of such ponds or basins can be built one next to the other to accommodate collections of several different species. The illustration (Fig. 6) shows how such ponds should be built. Care must be taken to see that the edges of the pond slope gradually and easily to the water, otherwise the ducks cannot 'land' in comfort. Little ducklings may die if they cannot climb to firm soil easily and, strange as it may seem, they will drown if they do not come onto dry land at regular intervals.

An island can be created in a small pond without much trouble; or even a floating island on which a breeding box can be placed. Given the necessary planting, this soon becomes quite effective and tasteful. A rustic plank can be used to connect it to dry land. A little skill and a great deal of imagination are needed to develop these water gardens in an artistic and natural manner. All kinds of ideas can be gathered when visiting zoos and aviaries in parks. There are also magazines and periodicals wholly or partly devoted to water-fowl, and the addresses of the publishers can readily be ascertained. In case of difficulty the addresses can be obtained of other fanciers who will be only too happy to help with advice.

FIG 5 *On land adjoining natural water, runs as illustrated above can be constructed. If the available ground does not actually adjoin the water, the same effect can be achieved by digging a trench from the water to each run.*

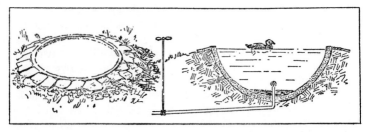

FIG 6 *The construction of an artificial pond requires considerable thought, especially as regards drainage. Choose a raised site and surround the pond with a broad path of flagstones which will prevent the ducks carrying in soil on their feet and thus fouling the water. The right-hand drawing shows how the drainage can best be arranged. The outlet should be covered with fine mesh wire to prevent the outflow from becoming choked with debris. The top of the pipe should also project about 4 in. above the bottom of the pond to prevent mud being drawn into it when emptying. When the water has been drained, the mud can be removed and the pond thoroughly cleaned.*

The making of an artificial pond presents some difficulties but here, too, success can be achieved even without the help of craftsmen. Asphalt paper, made of several layers of stout paper bonded together with bitumen, is often used and will last for years. The pond must have smooth and gradually sloping sides and a level base so that each width of the paper lies quite flat and overlaps. Many people, however, prefer to use a more permanent material such as concrete and a mixture of 1 part cement to 3 parts of fine gravel and sharp sand gives good results. After the excavating has been completed, the soil must be stamped down firmly and a layer of ash or rubble stamped in. It is of the utmost importance to incorporate some system of draining the pond. A drainpipe should be placed in position first so that the opening is in the exact centre of the pond, at its deepest point and the exposed end should be covered by a tin to prevent it from becoming blocked when the cement is being laid. The pond need not be deeper than 16–20 in. in the centre, and the slope should be gradual. The edge should be an inch above the surrounding ground and be at least 10 in. wide. Around the pond a fairly wide walk should be laid of flagstones, tiles or concrete. This ensures that the ducks do not continually carry earth into the water and thus muddy it unduly. The drainpipe must be set in concrete consisting of one part of cement to one of sand; otherwise there will be every chance of leakage. It should be closed with a tight-fitting rubber plug, attached to a chain (like a bath stop). The diameter of the pond should be at least 8–9 ft. This will be enough for 2 or 3 ducks.

Round ponds are most easily fashioned from concrete. Rectangular ones can be made quite well with asphalt paper but when it is empty it should not be walked on, as asphalt paper damages easily. The use of this paper is recommended only for a pond without drainage. If concrete is used it need not be thicker than 4 in. It looks very simple and easy on paper, but it requires skill and, above all, patience to obtain a smooth surface and a nice level top edge. The draining-pipe must terminate somewhere in a drain or ditch. It is quite pretty and effective to make the pond on a level slightly higher than the surrounding ground and drainage will be much simpler.

Many different species of ducks which a fancier can keep do not need an elaborate shelter; they can stay out, summer and winter, provided they can find adequate cover under thick shrubbery. A simple pen is, however, also useful as some species prefer the extra seclusion thus provided, when laying. It will also provide good protection for the ducklings.

If it is desired to let the ducks roam about on an open lawn or meadow, this must be fenced off with wire netting about 2 ft high.

FIG 7 *Movable duck pen which can be transferred to fresh ground daily. Protected against the weather on one side by felt.*

FIG 8 *Nest box for Mandarin or Carolina Ducks. Raised on a post about 30 in. above the ground with a 'ladder' consisting of a plank on which slats have been nailed to enable the duck to climb up to the nest.*

The wings of the ducks must be clipped. Most ducks eat a lot of grass, all manner of insects, slugs and snails, and so on. Species specially recommended as ornamental are the Carolina and the Mandarin. Unlike most other ducks, they normally nest in holes in trees. Their breeding boxes should therefore be raised well above ground level. It is quite a good plan to secure the box to a tree branch.

There are many other species which can be kept, such as the Bahamas, various kinds of Teal, White Call Ducks, Rosybills, and Tufted Ducks.

The Bahamas and Rosybills cannot be left without shelter during the winter. In a period of severe frost they should be kept in a shed, barn or stable where a thick layer of straw has been spread for them and where they can always find a supply of fresh drinking water. Their food and drinking troughs must be close together as the ducks take a bill full of food and dip it in the water in order to swallow it more easily.

Most species will breed in confinement. Boxes covered with branches of trees or bunches of twigs and heather should be placed on the ground and a layer of straw should be put inside each box. The ducks will soon find the boxes and when laying commences, a daily check should be kept and the eggs collected and replaced by nest eggs until the whole clutch is complete. When the duck starts covering the eggs with down, good results may be looked for. The eggs should be replaced in the nest and the duck will then start incubating. When the ducklings have hatched, the mother and her young should be placed in a small run with a little pond. The ducklings should be pinioned at once by clipping off the tip of one wing with sharp scissors. At this early age the operation will cause no pain or bleeding.

Boiled and mashed potatoes, stale bread, bran, maize meal and some barley meal make excellent duck food, well mixed with charcoal, grit and lime. The addition of some fish meal is also good.

Newly-bought ducks must be inspected carefully before they are let loose to see if they are healthy and have been pinioned. This is particularly important if they are to swim about in a large pond where it will not be so easy to retrieve them. It is, however, advisable to set a trap cage, in which the ducks should be regularly fed. Catching them will then present no difficulty; all that is needed is to scatter the food and quietly wait until they have entered the cage.

Apart from allowing the duck to hatch her own eggs, there are various methods of rearing the young. The eggs can be hatched by a broody hen. If this method is employed the one difficulty is to ensure that the ducklings have enough oil on them to make their down waterproof, as a hen cannot cover them with enough natural oil before they enter the water, whereas a duck will carefully grease her young before going onto the water with them.

The hen should be housed in a roomy run with the ducklings, in such a way that the latter can get into a second compartment where their rearing food is placed. This second compartment should be separated from the first by a wide meshed partition; the ducklings can easily slip through this but the hen cannot follow and eat their special food. The run should be movable and placed on a fresh piece of turf every day.

It is different again when the ducks' eggs are hatched in an incubator. The ducklings must then be placed in a brooder and the temperature kept constant during the first few days at 90°–95° F. (32°–35 °C). The first food and drinking water as well should be offered 24 hours after they are hatched. The ducklings will soon learn to eat if a little food is put on their beaks and the beak then held in water. It is beneficial also to allow a few ducklings which are a day or two older to run with them to teach them by example to feed. A layer of good dry sharp sand makes an excellent floor covering. If a connecting pen is placed outside the brooder the ducklings will soon learn to run to it and back again. They also learn quickly to run outside and gradually the temperature in the brooder can be lowered until they no longer need artificial warmth, but the lowering of the temperature must of course be governed to some extent by weather conditions. The ducklings should always have a dry surface on which to run about.

Mandarin and Carolina Ducks have different breeding and rearing habits. To achieve success with them, every breeding pair should be housed in a separate wire-covered aviary and supplied with a gangway or ladder to the raised entrance of the nest box, which should have an entrance hole 5 in. in diameter. A branch of a tree may be used for the gangway. It is preferable to let these ducks retain their full wings. Thick roosting perches should be supplied where they will sleep. Carolina Ducks start laying as early as April, usually 7–8 eggs in a clutch, which will take 31 days to hatch.

The Mandarin Duck will usually lay a little later, in April, and will sit for 30 days. The eggs may be hatched in an incubator or under a bantam hen, but it is certainly as well and much more interesting to let mother duck rear her own young. In addition to good rearing food, the ducklings should be given some mealworms and ants' eggs, with finely chopped green food. Crushed wheat should form the staple content of the diet later on.

# 6  AVIARIES FOR PARROTS AND PARRAKEETS

All members of the parrot family are 'carpenters' and even Budgerigars and other small Grass Parrakeets will quickly reduce softwood perches to matchwood and will damage or destroy all shrubs and growing plants. The larger parrakeets, parrots and cockatoos will attack all woodwork in the aviary and the ordinary light gauge wire-netting is quite inadequate to resist their powerful beaks.

Enclosures for the larger species are therefore better constructed of heavy gauge chain link wire on a frame of metal tubes or angle iron. This form of construction is of course more expensive and as the aviaries must be large, the total cost will be considerable. If several pairs are to be kept for breeding purposes it is preferable, and in most cases essential, to house each pair separately and it may then be found more convenient to construct a range of uniform aviaries with a service passage running along the back of the shelters from which food and water can be supplied without entering each enclosure and with a minimum of disturbance to the inmates.

Providing sufficient length is available to ensure that the birds can obtain plenty of exercise flying from end to end, it is not necessary that the enclosures should otherwise be very large; a width of 3 ft and a height of 6 ft will be sufficient but the flights should not be less than 8–10 ft long. In addition simple shelters should be provided about 3 ft by 4 ft and of the same height as the flights, with windows at the back to provide plenty of light. The light is essential as birds will not enter a dark shelter even in the worst weather conditions. The front of the shelter should be entirely enclosed with the exception of an entrance for the birds, placed near the top and about 12 in. wide and 18 in. high, with a sliding door which can be used to shut the birds in at night, should the weather be very severe during the winter months. The wooden frame of this entrance hole should be protected with sheet metal to prevent the birds from eating it away. It will not, of course, be possible to shut the birds in the shelter when they are nesting, as breeding operations are usually more successful when the nest boxes are in the open flight. Some birds have a tendency to roost hanging on the wire-netting and this must be discouraged, otherwise they may be injured by owls or prowling cats during the night, or they may lose their toes should an unexpected sharp frost occur.

Food and water should always be given in the shelters, not only as a convenience to the fancier but also to encourage the birds to enter freely of their own accord. Once they are accustomed to using the shelter little difficulty will be experienced in shutting them in when this becomes necessary.

The cocks of most breeding pairs become very aggressive during the nesting season and will often attempt to fight their neighbours through the wire dividing the enclosures or to attack young birds which may happen to alight on the wire. Serious injuries to toes and beaks may be inflicted and it is therefore a great advantage to have the partitions of double wire with at least an inch space between. This of course will add to the initial cost of the aviaries but may well prove to be an economy in the long run if it saves valuable stock birds from being mutilated.

There is little point in planting shrubs in the flights as these will almost certainly be destroyed by the birds, but turf may be laid and various seeds such as canary, sunflower and rape grown which will provide a useful addition to the diet and will be greatly appreciated, especially when young birds are being reared.

Shallow baths should be provided in the flights although some species will seldom enter water, preferring to bathe by running through wet grass and foliage after a shower of rain. During a prolonged period of drought the birds greatly enjoy an occasional spraying. The grass growing in the flights should be kept well watered, especially at a time when eggs are being incubated, as the necessary degree of humidity in the nest box is maintained by moisture carried in by the birds when their plumage is saturated, and will ensure satisfactory hatching of the eggs.

Natural branches are best for perches but the fancier must be prepared to renew these at frequent intervals as the birds will industriously remove all foliage and bark and will eventually destroy the wood. They are particularly fond of fresh pine or fir branches and there is no doubt that the fresh wood contains much of value to the health of the birds and also the constant gnawing helps to sharpen their beaks and to prevent them from becoming overgrown.

# 7 NEST BOXES FOR PARROTS AND PARRAKEETS

With only one known exception, the Quaker Parrakeet, *Myiopsitta monachus*, all parrot-like birds nest in holes, most species selecting hollow branches or tree trunks. A few burrow into the ground or into termite nests, or use cavities between rocks as nesting sites and the nesting habits of these will be discussed in detail when describing the species concerned.

Of the hole nesters only the African Lovebirds, *Agapornis*, use any nesting material and they fill the nesting hollow completely with bark which they strip off growing twigs and branches. Through this mass of material they force an entrance tunnel to the nesting cavity in which the eggs are deposited, often pulling the materials together and closing the tunnel after they have entered. High humidity is required to ensure successful hatching of Lovebirds' eggs and it is therefore as well to place a handful of wet moss or well-soaked peat in the bottom of their nest boxes and to supply them with a large bundle of willow twigs from which they can strip the green bark which contains an exceptionally high percentage of sap.

None of the other species will accept any form of nesting material. They merely scrape a shallow cavity in the rotten wood chips or other debris at the bottom of the nesting hole and the eggs are laid in this cavity. Budgerigar breeders have devised a very practical form of nesting box with a removable base of thick wood in which

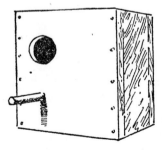

FIG 9 *Wooden nest box with wooden base made from a solid board. Both Budgerigars and Lovebirds readily make use of this type of box. A layer of sawdust can be put in the bottom so that the eggs will keep together when the hen is incubating and will not roll into the corners. Lovebirds will completely fill the box with green twigs and bark. The top of the box is removable to allow inspection of the eggs and young.*

a cavity of suitable size has been chipped out. A layer of damp sawdust in the bottom prevents the eggs from being broken and the cavity prevents them from being rolled into a corner and ensures that they keep together where they can be properly covered by the sitting hen. Whether natural hollow logs or artificial wooden nest boxes are used, they should all have such a cavity and halved coconut shells are sometimes used for this purpose, the space between them and the sides of the box being filled with cement or firmly packed with clay. A more natural base can be made by fitting a thick turf in the bottom of the box, with the grass downwards. A suitable hollow can be pressed into this with the knuckles and the turf kept sufficiently damp to ensure reasonable humidity.

Nesting operations will be more successful if the nest boxes are in the open flight, in a light but reasonably secluded position and with the entrance hole facing north. Large boxes are best fixed on top of a post or tree trunk. Smaller boxes can be hung on the wire or against the outside of the shelter but in this position they should be partly screened with fir branches or bunches of heather.

They should not be exposed to the full heat of the sun as this will tend to dry the atmosphere in the nest and make hatching more difficult. Also, as the young birds grow and begin to fill the nest the

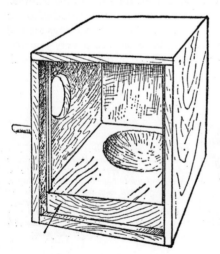

FIG 10 *This nest box with removable bottom has the advantage that it can more easily be cleaned. A brood of young birds soon make the nest foul and the removable bottom can be emersed in hot water to which a little Lysol or other disinfectant has been added before a second clutch of eggs is laid.*

temperature inside the box would become unbearably high and might well suffocate them. The wood used for the construction of the boxes should be of 1 in. thickness as this will help to maintain an equitable temperature and as an added precaution a number of small ventilation holes should be drilled towards the top. The entrance hole should also be near the top and if the box is deep, some form of ladder must be provided on the inside to enable the birds to climb in and out. This may be in the form of wooden slats nailed horizontally across the inside below the entrance hole or wire-netting tacked flat to the inside surface will serve the purpose. It is also advisable to fix a perch on the outside of the box just below the entrance hole as the cocks of some species like to stand guard over the entrance to their nest when their hen is sitting and will also feed her during the in-cubation and brooding period.

For powerful birds such as Cockatoos and Amazons the edge of the entrance hole should be protected with sheet metal, otherwise they will chew the wood away until the whole front of the box is destroyed.

The size of the nest boxes must of course vary according to the size of the species for which they are required but the following measurements may serve as a rough guide:

### Internal measurements

| | |
|---|---|
| Budgerigars | 6 in. × 6 in. × 9 in. deep. |
| Lovebirds | 8 in. × 8 in. × 12 in. deep. |
| Grass Parrakeets, Cockatiels and other species of similar size | As for Lovebirds. |
| Rosellas | 8 in. × 8 in. × 18 in. deep. |
| Ringnecks and other long-tailed species | 9 in. × 9 in. × 24 in. deep. |
| Amazon Parrots | 18 in. × 18 in. × at least 36 in. deep. |
| Cockatoos | As for Amazons. |

When first introduced to a new aviary most of the parrots and parrakeets are shy and timid and take some time to settle down sufficiently to commence nesting. The larger species also take some years to reach maturity and the fancier should not be discouraged therefore if his birds fail to nest in the first year or two.

# 8   CAGES AND STANDS FOR PARROTS

Very few of the parrakeets are suitable as cage pets; they are active and restless by nature and if confined in a small space usually damage their plumage and become over-fat and unhealthy. The large, short-tailed parrots such as Amazons and African Greys however and some of the cockatoos are of a more placid disposition and in a wild state spend more of their time clambering amongst the branches of forest trees than their smaller and more active relatives. Further-more nearly all those which are imported to Europe have been taken from the nest when quite small and hand reared by natives, con-sequently they are usually tame and confiding.

They require a large, all metal cage with stout, hardwood perches and such cages are readily obtainable. They are somewhat costly but as they are to provide a home for a bird which is itself expensive, once it has been decided to spend twenty to thirty guineas on a parrot no economy should be exercised on its living accommodation as it will probably be a life-long companion and give great pleasure to its owner provided it is well looked after.

Brass cages, however beautiful or antique, should be avoided as verdigris will form on this metal sooner or later. When the bird climbs round the cage the verdigris is sure to get into its beak and as it is very poisonous this will cause sickness and may even prove fatal.

In order to maintain first-class condition the birds require more exercise than they are able to obtain in the cage. A climbing pole and cross perch should therefore be kept beside the cage and the birds allowed out daily to clamber on it and stretch their wings. At the same time a shallow pan of water should be available in which they can take a bath if they feel so inclined. If, as is sometimes the case, they refuse to bathe, they should occasionally be sprayed with tepid water which they will thoroughly enjoy.

The cage should be kept on a stand, in good light and away from draughts and should never be below eye level. It should be partly covered with a cloth at night as the bird will sleep more comfortably with this added protection from cold and draught.

Large, long-tailed parrots of the Macaw family are sometimes kept on 'T' perches or parrot stands, to which they are secured by a light chain attached to one leg. This however is a most unsatisfactory method of keeping any bird and they are really only suitable as inmates of a large aviary.

## 9 MIXED COLLECTIONS OF PARROT-LIKE BIRDS

With one exception the parrot-like species are not good mixers and although it is possible to keep certain species together, provided there are no hens present, there is always the risk that fighting may occur which will lead to birds being seriously injured or maimed. The various species of Rosellas are particularly spiteful and it is far better to provide separate accommodation for pairs of these birds even if this necessitates limiting the size of the aviaries to quite small dimensions. If a really large enclosure is available, a collection of various species of Amazons may be kept together as these large parrots are usually more docile except when nesting, but their voices are harsh and their continuous screeching may well lead to trouble with neighbours.

Lories and Lorikeets should always be kept in pairs or singly, in separate aviaries. Normally these birds roost in nest boxes and any attempt to mix the species will certainly lead to trouble for they are spiteful at all times and are certain to quarrel over the selection of roosting sites.

Most of the Lovebirds may be kept in colonies provided there is ample room in the aviary and adequate nesting facilities are provided. It is advisable to supply at least twice as many nest boxes as there are pairs of birds. If the species are to be mixed it will be difficult to prevent the production of hybrids as most of the species interbreed freely. The least suitable for a mixed collection are the Peach-faced.

The one exception is the Cockatiel which seldom, if ever, interferes with any other bird in the aviary, however small or large it may be.

It is, in fact, so peaceful and inoffensive that it will seldom attempt even to defend itself against attack and the fancier's one concern must therefore be to ensure that it is not subjected to persecution by other inhabitants of the aviary.

There is, of course, no objection to a pair of parrakeets being kept with birds of an entirely different species and a pair of pheasants, quail or doves make suitable companions and add greatly to the interest of the collection. Small seed-eaters may also be included with safety but the fancier must bear in mind the destructive habits of the parrakeets and it will be found necessary to constantly renew the branches and other small perches in the aviary otherwise the seed-eaters will have no perching or roosting facilities and may suffer from exposure, especially on cold nights.

## 10  THE EGG AND FECUNDITY

Good physical condition of the parent birds as well as good heredital predisposition and maturity, stimulated by the hormones, are essentials for the production of fertilized and viable eggs.

The weather and the temperature also have considerable influence. During the cold weather the sperm is less active. Sunlight has a beneficial effect on the reproductive organs. A period of bad, dull weather during the breeding season may well prove to be the cause of poor fertility.

We mate a pair of birds usually without consideration for their own choice. All kinds of factors influence us. We desire a particular colour or form in the young, and we select two birds which we think will produce the desired results. But sometimes a bird will not accept the partner selected. Some hens will definitely refuse to mate with the cock chosen for them and will show their preference for another.

It may happen occasionally that the cock is sterile. This we can determine if we have placed him with several hens in succession without obtaining fertile eggs.

To fertilize the eggs it is not essential to leave the cock with the hen all the time. The cock's sperm may be retained by the hen for some time and will serve to fertilize a whole clutch of eggs. The cock must be with the hen before the eggs are so far developed that albumen has formed around the yolk. As soon as this has happened fertilization is no longer possible. For this reason it sometimes happens that the first egg may be infertile.

Birds in bad physical condition will often lay infertile eggs, especially hens which are too fat, and steps must be taken to improve their condition.

A change of mate for canaries, pheasants and other birds often proves effective. The cock should be placed in the centre cage or aviary of a set of three, with his hens in the adjacent cages. He should spend one day with one hen, then be put back in his own cage for a day's rest, and let into the other hen's cage on the third day. One mating can be sufficient for the whole clutch.

During the rearing of the young the cock may be taken away, at least if he does not show any inclination to help the hen. It is only after a fortnight that a hen which has been feeding young comes into season again. Then the cock should be admitted to fertilize the next clutch.

To ascertain whether the eggs are fertile, they should be 'candled' after a week. (This is easily done by making a small round hole in the bottom of a fruit tin. Place a lamp inside the tin, lay the egg on the hole, and then it can easily be seen whether the egg is fertile or not.)

As well as the causes already mentioned for the non-development of the embryo, dryness may also prevent successful hatching. Nest pans hung against a wooden wall exposed to fierce rays of the sun can dry up. Spraying the eggs with tepid water may sometimes help. If the hens are encouraged to bathe regularly they will carry sufficient moisture back on their plumage to the eggs.

During the first few days of incubation the eggs should be safe-guarded against cooling. Care must be taken that the hen leaves the nest as little as possible, and all interference with the nest should really be avoided, unless the hen is particularly tame and remains sitting or returns immediately the inspection is completed.

The development in the egg demands constant uninterrupted

warmth from the commencement of incubation. Once the embryo starts developing it gives off heat itself and cooling for short periods each day cannot hurt.

There may be various reasons why a hen leaves the eggs after she has been incubating for some days. Sometimes the eggs are infertile.

If we find that the hen leaves her eggs regularly or sits restlessly, there is a possibility that lice are bothering her. Thanks to all kinds of insecticides, lice can be combatted easily, but prevention is better than cure and all possible hiding places should be sprayed with a liquid or powder insecticide. This spraying must be repeated immediately before the eggs are laid.

A living egg has a glossy shell and the carbonic acid gas is expelled and oxygen taken in through the shell. Therefore the eggs must be kept scrupulously clean. Parrakeet nest boxes which have been soiled should be regularly cleaned. If the pores of the egg shell are clogged, the embryo will die. The breeding pens of bird rooms in which birds are nesting should be regularly aired so that plenty of oxygen is available. Windows must be kept open.

If all this advice is followed, it should be unnecessary to place the eggs in tepid water the day before the chicks are expected in order to make the shells more friable; nor should it be necessary to help the chick by chipping the shell. Birds which cannot come out of the egg unaided usually prove to be weaklings. Should the embryo die before it is due to come out of the egg, the fault may usually be traced to lack of condition of the parent birds, with the result that the eggs did not contain a full compliment of the essentials of life.

Should the birds be supplied with insufficient lime, grit, cuttle fish and minerals, the shell may be too thin and will soon crumble. The diet should contain everything necessary for the formation of sound eggshells.

Fertilizing can be assisted by supplying food containing activating agents such as wheat germ oil or seeds which have a stimulating effect on the cock.

The hen must have a period of rest after completing a few clutches; if not, she may become exhausted and die. So far as possible birds which have bred out-of-doors during the summer should not be kept together as pairs during the winter, and certainly not if they are to winter indoors in a warm room. Late hours and artificial lighting are bad; they upset the normal period of rest and stimulate the development of gland secretions. The cocks may even start some sort of singing; if so, they will be unable to achieve their full song the following spring. A long winter rest reduces the glandular working to a minimum and induces a powerful stimulant in the spring.

Yeast and powdered seaweed have a beneficial effect on the breeding urge; one teaspoonful of either or both may be mixed in the food once a week during the early spring.

It is better and cheaper to purchase reliable breeding stock than to use all kinds of remedies and concoctions in an effort to induce birds of poor stamina to breed.

# 11  MUTATIONS

Attempts are continually being made to breed or produce new forms or colour varieties of animals and of plants. Wild animals do show unusual differences, but it is rarely that these are passed on to succeeding generations. Albinos are often met with in bird life, but a fixed strain of albinos has never been found in a natural state. Wild parrots showing colour variations have been found in their natural surroundings. The Indian Ring-necked Parrakeets have produced birds with diluted colours, while a blue variety of the Quaker Parrakeet has been found, and so on.

Only when such birds can be induced to breed in captivity under strict control can some influence be brought to bear on the reproduction of mutations. Accommodation, diet and such things undoubtedly exercise a great influence, and may affect the heredity colour factor, whereas 'natural selection' always tends to reject the abnormal.

It is only as a result of Mendel's experiments that the laws governing mutations and heredity have been discovered and although we are only at the beginning of these discoveries, we have been able to apply the laws to our advantage. We are at least able to fix for a further generation a past mutation, such as a difference in colour, length, size of wings or length of tail. We know that children take after their parents, grandparents and even earlier ancestors. Resemblances exist not only in character but also in physical properties such as curly hair, a special shape of nose, the historically famed Habsburg lip and so on. But how these hereditary properties are passed on in the human race is but vaguely known. In this book we are concerned only with birds, and much is still but vaguely understood. Unending experiments still have to be performed before our knowledge becomes complete.

Nevertheless, we have a certain number of 'rules' at our disposal and with the aid of these we are able to obtain good results. Some French professors have made a notable advance. By injecting hormone from one species of duck into another species, such a change has occurred in the chromosomes that a third species has been created. This knowledge is, of course, of the utmost importance to plant and animal breeders and has long been used in experiments with poultry. Egg production has been increased, broodiness diminished, liability to disease reduced, and so on.

This book is not a thesis on the laws of Mendel, nor will its pages be filled with calculations and hereditary formulae. There are books available which go deeply into the matter, and articles have frequently appeared in various periodicals. Here we shall deal only with mutations which will be commonly met with by fanciers, that is heterochrosis or 'change of colouring'.

We have to distinguish between the discoloration of birds in cages or aviaries, so-called loss of colour, and a real change in pigmentation. The latter first appears in the nest feathers of young birds and is therefore the result of hereditary factors, whereas the former usually appears in adult birds following their first moult in captivity and is more often than not the result of incorrect feeding or a lack of certain essential elements in the food supplied. Too little green food may have been supplied, not enough minerals given, insufficient live insects, or other faults in diet. Scarlet Ibis in captivity often turn to a pale pink, and it is only when they are allowed to paddle in a pond teeming with water fleas and other live crustacea and given green grass to walk on, that they recover their vivid colouring. Canary fanciers know many a trick to get their orange-reds or red-oranges intensely red, whether by feeding them colour food, supplying them with Scotch kale and grated carrot, or giving them carrot juice to drink. It is possible to get a beautiful gloss on the birds by feeding them seaweed powder. Many things can still be done to regain the brilliant colouring which the birds always have when wild.

Obviously, all this has nothing to do with heredity, though it is possible that birds with faded plumage may in due course produce descendants with paler colouring, due to the fact that they lack the essential elements to pass on to their offspring.

A mutation is a derangement which occurs suddenly in the combination of the chromosomes of cock and hen, at the moment when the sperm unites with the egg cell. This derangement can, of course, occur in any of the chromosomes, but for the moment we are concerned only with those which are the bearers of one or more colours. Among the chromosomes are those responsible for the determination of the sex and it is now known that certain colour factors are linked to these sex chromosomes. It will therefore be evident that special colours or colour properties are tied inseparably to the sex chromosomes, and as a result only one sex, say the male, can carry the specific colour. This connection between certain colours and the sex chromosomes is known as sex-linked heredity.

Theoretically, all colours are built up from the three primary colours, yellow, blue and red. Black and white are not colours but are the outward indication of the intensity of certain colour combinations. For instance, the combination of yellow, red and blue in correct proportion produces the appearance of black. When one of these three colours is present in abnormally high or low proportion, we are faced with a heterochrosis, i.e. the production of a different colour.

The parrot types mostly show a derangement in the development of the blue colour, called the blue pigment.

If the blue pigment is entirely absent, then green, which is a combination of blue and yellow, is reduced to pure yellow and any areas which were pure blue become colourless, i.e. white. Black will also disappear since blue is a constituent of black. Any red areas however will remain unaltered since red is a fixed and unalterable pigment.

Experiments have shown that the development of one colour or another can be influenced by certain light rays. We are only at the beginning of this domain. *Lutinism* is most frequently met with

D

among the African and Asiatic Parrots, only sporadically among Australians. A peculiarity is that the eyes in the case of pure lutinism are red. Birds with red eyes are troubled by bright sunlight and their sight is generally weak.

We all know yellow birds which do not have red eyes but black, and this is therefore not a pure lutinism but a *Panthochromism*. Now it does happen that birds sometimes change colour when adult, for instance losing the blue pigment, and furthermore this does not return after a moult. This may be an indication of age, and has nothing to do with mutation; for a mutation is a permanent factor, evident from birth.

Similar to lutinism is *Albinism* where in addition to the blue, the yellow pigment has also dropped out. As a result both pigments responsible for green colouring are absent, and no colour remains; the bird then appears pure white. There are several examples among the parrots, for example a Roseate Cockatoo, dead white in colour with only a pink crest.

When the yellow only drops out it is called *Cyanthinism*. Green without yellow becomes blue, yellow becomes white, black stays black. Examples of this are frequently seen in *Agapornis personata,* which becomes blue and white and has a red bill. Blue Quaker Parrakeets have been found in their native habitat. These mutations have also been found in the Indian Ring-necked Parrakeet, the Amazon – and the Dwarf Parrot.

Of frequent appearance is *Melanism*, i.e. turning black. Although this may occur once in a while as a mutation, it is generally an appearance due to old age or incorrect feeding. Tiger Finches fairly frequently show this deviation, while pheasants are renowned for it.

*Erytrism*, becoming red, also occurs, but generally the red colouring is only partial. Some parrots develop splashes of red on different parts of the back or breast.

*Dilutism*, thinning down of colour appears repeatedly as a mutation with the Indian Ring-necked Parrakeets and the Red-rumped Parrakeet and with Budgerigars, the latter now being called Greywings.

In order to retain a mutation it is necessary to pair the young bird back with its father or mother. Birds which take more than a year to reach maturity, as for instance the Ring-necked Parrakeets, offer extra difficulties on this account and it may take years to build up a strain of lutinos of such a species. Added to this is the fact that the lutino factor is sex-linked, consequently lutinos resulting from the first generation will all be hens. If these hens are paired back to the father, which apparently carried the latent lutino factor, the resulting young should be 25% lutino sons and 25% lutino daughters, 25% normal daughters and 25% so-called 'split' lutino cocks, birds which look quite normal outwardly, but which can transfer the lutino factor to their daughters.

I would like to give an example of hereditary expectations. A cock has two male (X) chromosomes, i.e. the sex chromosomes are paired two of a kind, whereas a hen has only one male (X) chromosome and a female (Y) chromosome. When a mating takes place the two chromosomes of each parent separate and one X from the cock unites with the X from the hen, the other joining to the Y chromosome. Thus we have the following formula:

|   | X | Y |
|---|---|---|
| X | XX | XY |
| X | XX | XY |

Theoretically, therefore, cocks and hens will be produced in equal proportions. But we should not forget that in order to confirm this percentage, we should have the actual results of one hundred nests available. Moreover, there are individual variations the causes of which are unknown, but which have come to light in the course of experimental breeding. There are hens which always produce more daughters than sons, something which is, of course, met with in the human race as well. I have known Chinese Painted Quail which reared broods consisting mainly of hens, whereas exactly the reverse is claimed for this species, viz. that they always had an enormous excess of cocks. Insufficient notice has been taken of these deviations from the general rule, but I am certain that such individual differences would also be found in the case of canaries and parrakeets. if only the trouble were taken to register accurately all nesting results.

In spite of this handicap, which is somewhat detrimental to the theory, these formulae can be workable, provided the results are estimated correctly, viz. as 'expectations'. Should the proportion prove to be entirely different in the first nest, this does not prove the theory to be wrong and the balance may well be corrected by the results of a subsequent brood. If there is a nest of 6 youngsters of which 4 are hens and 2 are cocks, then the next nest may be expected to produce the inverted proportion, because finally as many cocks as hens will be born (except in individual instances as I have already pointed out).

Returning to the example of the lutino (sex-linked heredity), I would like to clarify this with a few formulae. As I said before, the lutino factor is tied to a sex chromosome, viz. the X factor which we will indicate as XI. If both the X chromosomes have the lutino factor then we obtain XI XI, that is a male lutino bird. The female lutino will then be XIY.

An XI is a male bird, which is 'split' for the lutino factor, but outwardly appears of normal colour. That he is outwardly normal tallies with the fact that 'normal' is dominant to lutino.

We now get the following expectations:

(1) Split lutino cock × normal hen.

|     | X   | Y   |                                |
| --- | --- | --- | ------------------------------ |
| XI  | XXI | XIY | therefore 25% split lutino cocks |
|     |     |     | 25% normal cocks               |
| X   | XX  | XY  | 25% lutino hens                |
|     |     |     | 25% normal hens.               |

It is *not* possible to recognize by the visible characteristics of the young males whether they are carriers of the hereditary lutino factor or not! It is only by experimental matings that we can learn this. In these crossings we use two lutino hens and theoretically there are therefore now present two possibilities:

(2) Split lutino cock × lutino hen:

|      | XI   | Y   |
| ---- | ---- | --- |
| XI   | XIXI | XIY |
| X    | XXI  | XY  |

therefore 25% lutino cocks
25% split lutino cocks
25% lutino hens
25% normal hens.

or (3) normal cock × lutino hen:

|      | XI   | Y   |
| ---- | ---- | --- |
| X    | XXI  | XY  |
| X    | XXI  | XY  |

therefore 50% split lutino cocks
50% normal hens.

The difference is now obvious. From pairing number 3 only outwardly normal birds make an appearance and we are then certain that the cock used lacks the lutino factor. In 2 we find lutino cocks as well as hens, while we are moreover certain that the other cocks all possess the factor, and are therefore split for lutino.

I have said before that in order to retain the mutation, it is essential to mate one of the offspring back to the parent bird, made clear again by example 2. The first lutino bird must have been a hen and her father must possess the factor, as her mother could not have possessed it. If we therefore mate the lutino daughter with her father we get the result as given in 2. If we cross the lutino sons and the lutino daughters with one another then we have fixed the mutation for then we get (4):

|      | XI   | Y   |
| ---- | ---- | --- |
| XI   | XIXI | XIY |
| XI   | XIXI | XIY |

therefore 50% lutino cocks
50% lutino hens.

In addition to the sex-linked heredity there is the dominant/ recessive heredity to be considered. Here the sex of the parent bird plays no part and the expectations are governed only by which colour is dominant and which recessive.

If we take as an example a green Budgerigar and a blue Budgerigar (both pure stock) then we find upon crossing these two, only green young will be produced from which it becomes evident that green is dominant and blue recessive. We do not give the birds the letters XX and XY, for we are not now concerned with sex chromosomes and we may now use the letters G for green (a capital letter to indicate that green is dominant) and b for blue (small type to indicate that blue is recessive):

|   | b | b (blue hen or cock) | |
|---|---|---|---|
| (Green Cock or Hen) | | | |
| G | Gb | Gb | 100% green birds all split |
| G | Gb | Gb | for blue |

If we cross the youngsters among themselves we get:

|   | G | b | |
|---|---|---|---|
| G | GG | Gb | 25% green birds (normal pure stock) |
|   |   |   | 50% green birds split for blue |
| b | Gb | bb | 25% blue birds (blue pure stock) |

There may be a similar number of cocks and hens, therefore theoretically speaking, one half of the percentages can be male and the other half female. It is most probable that the actual result per nest will show quite a different proportion. Here again the results should be based on 100 youngsters to give a true percentage. The difficulty remains that with these results we cannot differentiate by visual means the green pure stock birds from those which are split for blue, and it is only by further experimental pairing that this can be decided. I do not want to probe further into this matter for I could fill any number of pages with more theories. But there is a third hereditary possibility which I will mention, viz. the intermediary or average.

We must imagine that we are going to cross black and white. What kind of progeny shall we obtain? Red and white combination gives pink. Will black and white therefore produce grey? With these birds there are various factors which are intermediary hereditary. Budgerigars have a so-called dark factor, which may appear in normal or intense form or may be entirely lacking. According to the presence or absence of that factor associated with all colours of Budgerigars we find the so-called light, or middle or dark tones. As an example I shall take the blue Budgerigar. We have three variations, viz. sky blue, cobalt and mauve. The hereditary analysis of this colour will then be as follows:

Sky blue l = lacking of the dark factor = light.
Cobalt m = presence of the single dark factor = middle.
Mauve d = presence of both dark factors = dark.
l × d = 100% m; l × m = 50% l and 50% m; m × m = 25% l, 50% m and 25% d; m × d = 50% m and 50% d; d × d = 100% d; l × l = 100% l.
From this it follows that:
Sb (sky blue) × mauve gives 100% cobalt.
Sb × co (cobalt) = 50% Sb and 50% co;
co × co = 25% Sb, 50% co and 25% ma.
co × ma (mauve) = 50% co, and 50% ma;
ma × ma = 100% ma.
Sb × Sb = 100% Sb.

There are divers properties which are intermediary hereditary, others which are dominant hereditary and also factors which pass on both. It is only experimentally that it can be ascertained how a certain property, say a colour, is passed down. From the above it will be clear that hundreds of experiments are necessary in order to state *with certainty* any rule of heredity.

It may take years before a recessively hereditary mutation can be fixed, which will be plain from the following example:

|   | G | b |  |
|---|---|---|---|
| G | GG | Gb | 25% green |
|   |   |   | 50% green split for blue |
| b | Gb | bb | 25% blue. |

Both parents must have been split for blue, otherwise a blue bird could not have been produced. This blue bird is now paired back to one of its parents and then we obtain the following results:

|   | G | b |   |
|---|---|---|---|
| b | Gb | bb | 50% green split for blue. |
| b | Gb | bb | 50% blue. |

If there happens to be (theoretically an equal number of) blue cocks and hens then we can mate these among themselves and will obtain bb × bb = 100% bb.

Once we have nests of exclusively blue birds, then and only then can we speak of pure stock.

Everyone who intends to specialize in colour breeding must realize that a thorough study of the laws of heredity as at present known is essential. Without knowledge of these fundamental laws there will be failures. New colours and new varieties of birds are always being discovered. The birds obtained from a bird shop come from different breeders and the factors which they carry are often not obvious in their plumage. Guaranteed pure stock is to be obtained only from professional breeders who keep accurate records of pedigree without which serious work cannot be carried on. The birds are specially selected and paired, for reliable results can only be obtained when each pair is separately caged.

This branch of bird keeping is interesting and fascinating. Canaries, Budgerigars, Zebra Finches, Bengalese, Java Sparrows and many other species offer wide scope for experimental breeding.

## 12 THE INFLUENCE OF HORMONES

In the case of Pekin and Campbell Ducks, treatment with hormones has resulted in a regrouping of the chromosomes, and mutations have thus been obtained. This is of far-reaching significance; it is probably as important as splitting the atom and equally dangerous.

Not only can the outward appearance of a bird be changed by hormones, but also its character and behaviour. The application of various rays can also influence the working of the hormones, and it is now accepted that the action of sunlight partly determines the behaviour of animals and birds. The mating and breeding times are accompanied by many changes in the outward appearance and behaviour of birds; some, especially the cocks, assume a special breeding plumage, they display and perform dances, sometimes mock combats are staged, and the cocks start defending their breeding territory ferociously against intruders. The hens also change and become more aggressive and assertive. In addition to the influence exercised by the sun, unknown factors probably play their several parts and, by their periodical appearance, are responsible for the regularly recurring breeding instinct, which often disappears as suddenly as it appears.

The mystery of bird migration might well be explained along similar lines.

Experiments with hormone injections are not within the scope of the ordinary bird fancier. Thanks, however, to the observations of scientifically-minded bird owners, much has already been discovered about the influence of hormones on the behaviour of birds. Special attention has been focussed on the mating and breeding seasons.

If a mixed population has been housed for some time in a community aviary it will be found that there is a certain measure of regularity; one particular bird will always be the first to visit the freshly filled feed box and among birds of a particular variety (such as Canaries), a certain precedence is to be noted. This is more readily observed when a collection is restricted to one variety or species only. So long as there is no indication of breeding, it will be seen at feeding-time and particularly at roosting that one particular cock is given absolute precedence and that those coming after him do so in a certain sequence. During the breeding time, especially once the nests have been made and the eggs laid, a wholly new development can be observed. The hormone activation has taken place. The hen, which has a nest, immediately domineers all birds attempting to enter her breeding territory, and even more powerful intruders of other species are treated with ferocity.

With Canaries something happens to the hen during the breeding time by which, as it were, her character is changed. If dominance and the defence of the breeding territory is in the first place the task of the male, with his heightened sense of assertion, the hen also experiences a change and in her turn becomes assertive. Reasoning and premeditation cannot be assumed in the case of birds and their behaviour must therefore be attributed to a change in the functioning of the glands; in this instance the glands of internal secretions, or, in other words, the hormones. The ripeness of the hen engenders an important change in the internal organism; we might describe it as an 'egg laying cycle', stretching over a certain period of time. During this period it is possible even to note the progressive degree by which the hen defends her territory.

It is in the first place the male hormone which influences the assertiveness; this, in turn, regulates the question of precedence. From this it might be deduced that during the egg-laying cycle the glandular workings of the hen are affected in such a way that an appreciably higher proportion of male hormones is secreted, so much so that the hens during that period take precedence over the cocks. All this can be most easily observed in a bird room or indoor aviary, because in a more spacious outside flight the territorial frontiers are difficult to define. The greater accommodation and natural planting afford numerous and varied roosting facilities, and as a rule there are several feeding tables. Hence observation is difficult, if not well-nigh impossible. The reduction in living room strengthens, as it were, the effect of the characteristics; the breeding territory must be reduced and the defence intensified.

In a large flight the hen may even allow herself to be driven from her nest by intruders; this would never happen in a cage or indoor aviary.

Having proved the theory of the activated working of the male hormones, we must turn to the men of science for explanations. They have the opportunity to make experiments which, while beyond the reach of the fancier, will yield much valuable information. Nor should we forget that the observations of fanciers provided the scientists with a lead on which to base certain theories and conclusions.

Shoemaker made the following experiments with 'androgeen',

*i.e.* the male hormone. He determined the precedence of 6 Canaries by which three young birds came at the end of the line. He injected androgeen into these three young birds and thereby performed miracles, for they immediately became dominant over the adults and, moreover, started to sing.

A second experiment was carried out with Canaries kept in a cage with other birds by which they were absolutely dominated both at the food pots and in choice of roosting sites. After the injection the tables were turned and the Canaries dominated their former superiors.

So much for Shoemaker's experiments. No reference has been made to heredity in conjunction with glands. We know from experience that certain properties are hereditary, and it would be valuable to know if the domineering nature of some birds is also hereditary, for then it would be possible to pair birds with a view to fixing characteristics other than colour alone. As a rule, far too little attention is paid by breeders who are concerned only with colour production in Canaries and Budgerigars to other hereditary factors. It would be worth while, when drawing up a pedigree, to make special note of strong birds which can maintain their position. By injudicious breeding a great deal of damage can be done to the 'variety'. The Bengalese, for instance, in most cases have lost all desire to 'throw their weight about' and are therefore only suitable to breed in breeding pens or on their own.

More should also be known about the colour changes of certain birds during the breeding period, with the simultaneous appearance of domination. How far does the male hormone influence the change to red colouring of the Tiger Finch and of various Weavers when coming into breeding condition? Are these colours outward signs of the internal working of the hormones?

In closing this subject it should be pointed out that many failures with breeding Canaries and other domesticated birds can be traced to letting them breed when too young. It is only when these birds have attained a natural maturity by the influence of sunlight and are ready for pairing and fertilization that satisfactory results can be expected. Eggs which are infertile and dead-in-shell will not then occur. The physical condition of the birds, of course, has a major effect on fecundity and fertility.

Only when the fancier keeps fully alive to the varying needs and reactions of his birds will he get a glimpse of the 'life secrets'. His charges will then repay him with more youngsters, more gorgeous colouring and more song.

# 13 THE REMARKABLE BEHAVIOUR OF BIRDS

When a fancier has kept many species of birds for years, it will be not only the outward beauty or the beautiful song or colour which has left a permanent impression. More firmly fixed in the memory will be the observations of bird behaviour which he has been able to make.

Let us take, for example, the Whydahs, those birds which develop beautiful long tails annually as breeding time approaches. Their winter garb is usually a very simple striped drab-brown and buff feathering. By the yearly metamorphosis, not only is the outward appearance changed so remarkably, but also the character, transforming a normally quiet and peaceable bird into one which is exceedingly noisy and aggressive. The behaviour changes radically; not only are his own hens courted by his displays and dancing but also the hens of many other species which may share his aviary.

A peculiarity of several species of Whydah which has come to light only during the last few years is that they are brood parasitic on various foreign finches, and this makes the species still more interesting. The markings on the palate of newly hatched Whydahs correspond closely with those in the mouths of the foster parents' chicks, and in many cases even the immature plumage is very similar.

For every species of bird it would be possible to enlarge on the wonders of the courting and mating behaviour to a far greater length than is done in this book. There are good periodicals for bird fanciers appearing in many languages in which full and detailed observations are published and these help to build up a complete picture of this fascinating subject.

Reference must be made to the behaviour known as 'anting'. This is the strange habit of picking up live ants and placing them beneath the feathers. When watching birds, both in the wild, and also in aviaries, 'anting' has frequently been observed. This is practised by many different species of widely differing type and in all parts of the world. What is the explanation? Termites and ants have one thing in common – they all secrete formic acid. It therefore seems certain that this formic acid plays an important part in this mystery and that the birds instinctively take to 'anting' to attain some unknown benefit or pleasure from the influence of the acid on their skins.

Many different suggestions have been put forward to explain this behaviour. Some ornithologists suggest that it is the smell of formic acid which appeals to the birds but it seems highly improbable that birds go 'anting' just for a pleasant smell and nothing more. It has been repeatedly stated that starlings will settle deliberately in the smoke of a chimney, which must give their feathers a distinctly smoky smell. This, however, does not prove that they like this smoky smell but rather that the smoke serves a special need, *viz.*, the driving away of parasites which have attached themselves to the skin under the feathers.

Other ornithologists surmise that the birds rub the ants backwards and forwards under their feathers in order to rub off the heads containing formic acid, before eating the decapitated bodies. From this it might be deduced that the birds found the formic acid distasteful. Without doubting these observations, it must be stated that in most cases the ants were not eaten, but were later found dead where the 'anting' had taken place. The rubbing had indeed removed most of their heads, but this would seem to indicate that decapitation liberated the acid which was thus allowed to come into contact with the skin of the bird.

Yet another theory is that 'anting' is used as disinfectant to free the body from all manner of parasites; this has much to commend it, because ants have been pressed into service by people who wished to get rid of lice which have infested their clothes. During the Boer War soldiers were greatly troubled by lice; they placed their clothes over the nests of termites, and the termites removed every louse in a very short time. It is not known whether they killed the lice or only took them away for some ulterior motive such as to use them as 'milch cows'. Some lice exude juices which are fed to young ants. The de-lousing theory would seem to carry more weight were it not for the fact that quite young birds which certainly were free of parasites had been seen happily 'anting' which suggests that 'anting' may be compared to taking a sun, sand or water bath.

As a result of observations made in America of 'anting' by birds known to be always infested with lice, it has been suggested that the ants carry off the lice. But since bird lice are practically invisible to the naked eye that would seem to need further confirmation.

Birds take sun baths, water baths, sand baths, and smoke baths instinctively, seemingly without reason. It is difficult to trace the motives of these instinctive actions; in some way the birds must derive some mysterious virtue from these actions about which little is known.

There are, of course, certain birds which normally act as hosts to insects for some time, just as other species of birds are dependent for their livelihood on mammals with which they remain in constant contact. For example, the Buffalo or Tick Bird is always to be found on the buffalo, which it frees from parasites.

A remarkable example is provided by the Golden-winged Parra-keet. This builds its nest in the nests of termites, and the parasites which accumulate in the nesting hole remove and eat the excreta of the young. By this means the nest is maintained in a sanitary condition throughout the period it is occupied by the young birds. A similar case is that of the Hornbill which nests in hollow trees. The hen is, as it were, built in by the cock. The hole is filled up with mud until only a small slit remains through which the cock can feed the hen and through which the hen can eject a part of her excreta. The hen remains cooped up in her cell for fifteen weeks and as she is fed mainly on fruit it is beyond her power to clear the nest entirely of the accumulated waste herself. She is, however, aided in this task by a veritable multitude of insects which have been collected and brought to the nest by both birds beforehand and remain living there until they have finished their task. In one such nest hole 438 insects were found, mostly caterpillars. These lived in the nest, ate the excreta and kept the nest completely clean. This food induced in the caterpillars a kind of torpor, which made them inert and prevented their escape. During those 15 weeks it is estimated that the hen had eaten 24,000 fruits.

Reverting to the habit of 'anting', it has also been suggested that the birds which place ants under their feathers lay up a store of insect food, as the ants cling tightly to the birds by their powerful jaws and the birds are then able to consume them at their leisure. But this explanation appears rather far-fetched, because the behaviour of the birds invariably indicates that the 'anting' takes all their attention. What is more probable is the following explanation. A bird will rub a piece of apple under its feathers, and this would seem to indicate that the acid of the apple in some way or other causes a pleasant sensation to the skin. The same is probably the case with formic acid. The birds experience a pleasant sensation, puff out their feathers, insert the insects which they then proceed to rub to death, and so the formic acid comes into contact with their skin. If they are insect-eaters the birds sometimes devour the remains of the ants. Large numbers of parasites are rendered harmless by the action of formic acid or are driven away by it. If the birds are therefore troubled by lice, they will be relieved of these in the process of 'anting' but it is doubtful if the formic acid is applied specifically for this purpose. The results of 'anting' are analogous to those of sun bathing, ordinary bathing in water and smoke baths. The skin in stimulated and parasites are destroyed incidentally. For this remarkable behaviour the phrase 'ant-bathing' might well be coined.

# 14 ILLUSTRATIONS OF BIRDS

A complete index of the species, including illustrations, is on pages 224–230. They are listed under commonly accepted English names, Latin names, and alternative names.

In the captions to the illustrations, only the commonly accepted English names and Latin names are given.

1 **Bob White Quail** *Colinus virginianus*

2  **Chinese Painted Quail**  *Excalfactoria chinensis*

3 **Red-legged Partridge** *Alectoris rufa*

4 **Satyr Tragopan**
*Tragopan satyra*

5 **Temminck's Tragopan**
*Tragopan temmincki*

6 **Japanese
Green
Pheasant**
*Phasianus v.
versicolor*

7 **Himalayan
Monal**
*Lophophorus
impeyanus*

8
**Sonnerat's Junglefowl**
*Gallus sonnerat*

9
**Red Jungle-fowl**
*Gallus gallus*

10　**Black-breasted Kalij** (cock and hen)　*Lophura leucomelana lathami*

11　**Silver Pheasant**　*Lophura n. nycthemera*

12 **Edwards's Pheasant** *Lophura edwardsi*

13 **Swinhoe's Pheasant** *Lophura swinhoei*

14 **Bornean Crested Fireback** *Lophura i. ignita*

15 **Siamese Fireback** *Lophura diardi*

16 **Reeves's Pheasant** *Syrmaticus reevesi*

17 **Mikado Pheasant** *Syrmaticus mikado*

18 **Hume's Bar-tailed Pheasant** *Syrmaticus h. humiae*

19 **Lady Amherst's Pheasant** *Chrysolophus amherstiae*

20  **Golden Pheasant**  *Chrysolophus pictus*

21 **Bornean Great Argus** *Argusianus argus grayi*

22 **White Peacock** *Pavo cristatus alb.*

23 **Indian Blue Peacock** *Pavo cristatus*

24 **Peacock Displaying** *Pavo cristatus*

25 **Chinese Necklaced Dove**
*Streptopelia chinensis*

26 **White-crowned Pigeon** *Columba leucocephala*

27 **Triangular-spotted Pigeon** *Columba guinea*

28 **Diamond Dove** *Geopelia c. cuneata*

29 **White-bellied Dove** *Leptotila jamaicensis*

30  **Indian Green-winged Dove**  *Chalcophaps indica*

31 **Bronze-winged Pigeon**
*Phaps chalcoptera*

32 **Bleeding-heart Pigeon** *Gallicolum luzonica*

33 **Crested Bronze-winged Pigeon** *Ocyphaps lophotes*

34 **White-faced Tree Duck** *Dendrocygna viduata*

35 **Muscovy Duck** *Cairina moschata*

36 **Red-billed Tree Duck** *Dendrocygna a. autumnalis*

37 **Red-billed Tree Duck** with young

38  **Northern (Common) Pintail**  *Anas a. acuta*  (Drake)

39  **Northern (Common) Pintail**  *Anas a. acuta*  (Duck)

40 **Common Sheld-Duck** *Tadorna tadorna*

41 **Red-crested Pochard** *Netta rufina*

42  **Mandarin Duck**  *Aix galericulata*  and drake

43  **Carolina Duck**  *Aix sponsa*  and drake

44 **Hyacinthine Macaw**
*Anodorhynchus hyacinthinus*

45 **Red and Yellow Macaw**
*Ara macao*

46 **Lear's Macaw**
*Anodorhynchus leari*

47 **Illiger's Macaw**
*Ara maracana*

48 **Severe Macaw**  *Ara s. severa*

49 **Red and Blue Macaw**
*Ara chloroptera*

50   **Blue and Yellow Macaw**   *Ara ararauna*

51  **Noble Macaw**  *Ara nobilis cumanensis*

52 **Swainson's Lorikeet** *Trichoglossus haematod moluccanus*

53 **Purple-capped Lory** *Domicella domicella*

54 **Ornate Lorikeet** *Trichoglossus ornatus*

55 **Yellow-backed Lory** *Domicella garrula flavopalliata*

56 Head of **Great White Cockatoo**
*Kakatoe alba*

57 Head of **Lesser Sulphur-crested Cock**
*Kakatoe s. sulphurea*

58 Head of **Greater Sulphur-crested Cockatoo**
*Kakatoe g. galerita*

59 **Rose-crested Cockatoo**
*Kakatoe moluccensis*

60 **Greater Sulphur-crested Cockatoo**
*Kakatoe g. galerita*

61 **Bare-eyed Cockatoo** *Kakatoe s. sanguinea*

62  **Roseate Cockatoo**  *Kakatoe r. roseicapilla*

63  **Leadbeater's Cockatoo**  *Kakatoe l. leadbeateri*

64  **Cockatiel**  *Nymphicus hollandicus*

65 **Cactus Conure**
*Aratinga c. cactorum*

66 **Golden-crowned Conure**
*Aratinga a. aurea*

67 **Black-headed Conure** *Nandayus nenday*

68 **Red-headed Conure** *Aratinga erythrogenys*

69  **White-eared Conure**  *Pyrrhura l. leucotis*

70  **Brown-throated Conure**  *Aratinga pertinax aeruginosa*

71 **Yellow-headed Conure**   *Aratinga jandaya*

72  **Canary-winged Parrakeet**  *Brotogeris versicolurus chiriri*

73 **Tui Parrakeet** *Brotogeris st thoma st thoma*

74 **White-winged Parrakeet** *Brotogeris v. versicolurus*

75 **White-bellied Caique** *Pionites l. leucogaster*

76  **Black-headed Caique**  *Pionites m. melanocephala*

77  **Blue-fronted Amazon Parrot**  *Amazona a. aestiva*

78  **Yellow-naped Amazon Parrot**  *Amazona ochrocephala auro-palliata*

**Orange-bellied
Senegal Parrot**
*Poicephalus sene-
galus mesotypus*

80 **Festive
Amazon
Parrot**
*Amazona
f. festiva*

81 **Ruppell's Parrot** *Poicephalus rüppelli*

82 **Meyer's Parrot** *Poicephalus m  meyeri*

83  **Blue-headed Parrot**  *Pionus menstruus*

84  **Indian Ring-necked Parrakeet**
*Psittacula krameri manillensis*

85  **African Grey Parrot**
*Psittacus e. erithacus*

86 **Plum-headed Parrakeet** *Psittacula c.,cyanocephala* (cock and hen)

87 **Alexandrine Parrakeet** *Psittacula eupatria nipalensis*

**88 Barraband Parrakeet**
*Polytelis swainsonii*

89   **Princess of Wales Parrakeet**
*Polytelis alexandrae*

90 **Crimson-winged Parrakeet** *Aprosmictus e. erythropterus*

91   **Rock Peplar Parrakeet**   *Polytelis anthopeplus*

92 **Brown's Parrakeet** *Platycercus v. venustus*

93 **Green-winged King Parrakeet** *Alisterus c. chloropterus*

94 **King Parrakeet** *Alisterus s. scapularis*

95 **Madagascar Lovebird** *Agapornis c.*
*:cana* (cock and hen)

96 **Peach-faced Lovebird** *Agapor*
*roseicollis* (cock and hen)

97 **Abyssinian Lovebird** *Agapornis t. taranta* (cock and hen)

98 **Fischer's Lovebird** *Agapornis personata fischeri* (cock and hen)

99 **Masked Lovebird** *Agapornis personata personata* (cock and hen)

100 **Blue-crowned Hanging Parrot** *Loriculus g. galgulus*

101 **Pennant's Parrakeet** *Platycercus e. elegans*

**Stanley Parrakeet** *Platycercus i. icterotis*    103 **Turquoisine Grass Parrakeet**
*Neophema pulchella*

104 **Adelaide Parrakeet** *Platycercus adelaidae*

105 **Golden-mantled Rosella**   *Platycercus eximius cecilae*

106 **Mealy Rosella**   *Platycercus adscitus palliceps*

107 **Yellow Rosella**
*Platycercus flaveolus*

108 **Red-rumped Parrakeet**
*Psephotus h. haematonotus*
(yellow var.)

**109 Many-coloured Parrakeet**
*Psephotus varius*

110 **Elegant Grass Parrakeet**
*Neophema e. elegans*

111 **Red-rumped Parrakeet**
*Psephotus haematonotus*

**112 Barnard's Parrakeet**
*Barnardius b. barnardi*

13 **Bourke's Parrakeet** *Neophema bourkii*

114 **Splendid Grass Parrakeet** *Neophema splendida*

Opaline Medium Grey Budgerigar

Opaline Cinnamon Grey Green Budgerigar

117 Grey Green Budgerigar

118 Slate Cobalt Budgerigar

119 **Australian Dominant Yellow-faced Pied Blue Budgerigar**

# 15 DESCRIPTIONS AND CARE OF THE BIRDS

## QUAIL, PARTRIDGES, PHEASANTS

**Blue Quail** (Scaley Colin) *Callipepla squamata*
*Origin* Mexico, Arizona and western Texas.

10 in. *Cock:* Forehead and sides of head grey, ear coverts brown, elongated crown feathers brown with white tips, chin and throat yellow, neck, mantle, breast and sides light grey with black margins to the feathering giving appearance of scales. Towards breast ground colour becomes beige; markings on under parts are brown and angular. Upper parts and wings grey-brown, tail grey with narrow white margins along the outermost feathers. Beak horn-coloured, eye brown-black, legs horn-coloured. *Hen:* Throat markings different, feathers having dark shaft stripes.

These quail spend much of the day amongst the branches but at night find shelter and a roosting spot somewhere on the ground of the aviary under thick cover. Once they have grown used to aviary life, however, they will spend more time on the ground, searching for seed and insects, dust-bathing or lying in the sun. The greatest attention must be paid to keeping the birds free from insect pests, which not only attack the body and feathers, but get under the scales of the legs. The birds generally manage to keep themselves free of these pests provided they always have facilities to dust bath in a patch of dry sandy soil.

The aviary must also be well planted with thick low-growing shrubs to provide suitable nesting conditions.

Oats, hemp, millet, canary seed, maw and all kinds of grass and weed seeds should be made available. Soaked bread, insectivorous food, mealworms and grated raw meat, hard-boiled egg and finely cut-up green food should be given to supply variety in the diet.

General treatment is as for the Californian Quail (under). 10 to 12 eggs are usually laid and incubated by the hen in a slight hollow scratched in the ground under a shrub or in thick grass. Occasionally both parents will sit and the cock takes a full share in brooding the chicks. The young must be kept dry; they are very susceptible to damp. The eggs may also be successfully hatched in an incubator and a foster mother then used to rear the chicks; ants' eggs and rearing food and a shallow saucer of drinking water must be given. It is advisable to put small clean pebbles in the bottom of the saucer to give a footing for the young birds as they are inclined to drown themselves if they cannot easily scramble in and out.

E

**Californian Quail** *Lophortyx californica*
*Origin* West coast of N. America from
Oregon to southern California.

10 in. *Cock:* Forehead buff-white,
crown black, fading to chestnut, nape
and mantle grey, marked with white
and the feathers edged with black; eyebrow stripe white; throat, ear coverts
and fore neck black outlined with
white. Long, forward-nodding black
crest of club-like feathers. Back brown;
tail coverts olive-brown; tail dull
brown. Breast slate grey, remainder of
under parts buff, toning to chestnut in
centre, each feather distinctly outlined
with black. Eye hazel; beak, legs and
feet blackish. *Hen:* Has a short brown
crest and lacks the black and white
pattern on the head, which is dull grey-
brown.

These birds, being pugnacious, can
only be safely associated with large
birds, and should not be housed with
others of their own kind. A large well-
planted flight with much low shrubbery will soon make them feel at home.
They will choose a roosting-place high
up among the branches under the
covered-in part of the flight; housed
in this way they can remain in the
aviary summer and winter as they are
quite hardy. The covered-in portion
must, however, be waterproof, for the
birds are very sensitive to damp,
though not to cold.

Their maintenance does not call for
exceptional care; various seeds, some
crushed maize and oats, weed seeds;
possibly some insectivorous mixture,
live insects, mealworms and ants' eggs
will keep the birds in fine fettle. They
also like soaked bread.

Breeding will be successful only if
the birds are not disturbed. It is a good
plan to let a bantam hen hatch the eggs
and rear the young. The eggs can also
be placed in a small incubator and after
a fortnight put under the bantam hen.

Given a flight planted with grass,
clumps of heather and low-growing
shrubs and various quiet corners
under the shrubbery, the quail will
usually sit well and rear their own
young. The hen alone incubates. This
natural state of affairs is preferable to
incubators and foster-mothers.

An ideal rearing mixture is composed
of crumbs of rusk with hard-boiled
egg. In addition much green stuff and
live insects and ants' eggs should be
supplied. A small piece of meat
wrapped in a muslin bag can be hung
from the netting so that the flies which
will infest it can be snapped off by the
birds. Sand, grit and a piece of cuttle
fish must be given on the ground.
Finely minced raw meat is also excellent, and may be mixed with breadcrumbs.

The young birds can stay with their
parents all through the season, and need
be parted only in the following spring.

**Bob White Quail** (Virginian Colin)
*Colinus virginianus* Pl. 1
*Origin* USA

Nearly 9 in. *Cock:* Forehead black,
primaries black spotted with brown.
Neck feathers white with black and
brown spots. A black band runs from
eye to ear coverts, throat white. Remainder of the head white. Back
brown with black cross bands, remainder of upper parts olive-grey with
rust coloured spots. Red-brown breast,
merging into white on the belly with
black markings. Feathers of under tail
coverts have a black spot on a light
brown ground. Eye brown, bill dark
horn-coloured, legs blue-grey. *Hen:*
Has smaller markings on the head and
the spots, which are white on the head

of the cock, are browny-white on that of the hen.

These quail are bred in considerable numbers each year and young birds are usually available at moderate prices. They are well suited to our climate and make attractive inhabitants of an aviary, provided this is roomy. They may stay outside during both summer and winter. In addition to various seeds they will eat berries, green food and a number of insects. They prepare for breeding very early in the year. The hen makes a scrape in the sand and lines this with grass and leaves. The 12–16 eggs are hatched in 23 days, and both parents share in the care and rearing of the young. Ants' eggs and mealworms, also egg food and rearing food, are necessary. General treatment as for the Californian Quail.

**Chinese Painted Quail** (Blue-breasted Quail) *Excalfactoria chinensis* Pl.2
*Origin* Indian Peninsula, Ceylon, Indo-China and Formosa.

Smallest of the Quail, 4½ in. *Cock:* Upper parts brown mottled with black and with a blackish forehead. Cheeks white outlined by a black line extending from the beak, below the eyes and joining the black throat. Broad white crescent below black throat, extending backwards to base of ear coverts, bordered with black. Chest and flanks blue-grey; breast and belly deep chestnut. Eyes hazel, beak blackish, legs and feet yellow, claws black. *Hen:* Lacks the black and white markings of the head and upper breast, and also the blue-grey of the chest and flanks, and the chestnut breast. She is of a general dull brown colouring, mottled on the upper parts, paler on the breast.

Readily available, these quail are exceptionally good for keeping in a flight with small birds, as they nearly always remain on the floor. If kept in a flight, they must have a thickly planted corner, behind which the nesting shelters must be placed. It is good to scatter sharp river sand around this corner. The cock will defend his corner territory ferociously during breeding time against any birds which may be too inquisitive, hence it would be a mistake to introduce more than one pair of 'ground' birds in a flight, and certainly not a second pair of the same species. The nest is built simply with a little moss and blades of grass, or leaves; sometimes it will be only a depression in the soil.

Only the hen incubates, while the cock assiduously guards the nest. After 16 days the eggs are hatched and soon the hen will appear with her 6–8 young chicks; they will readily eat ants' eggs, finely cut up mealworms and green stuff. Fine seeds, millet, crushed oats, grass and weed seeds and some insectivorous mixture must be provided. Minced raw meat is also excellent, as well as biscuit crumbs and hard-boiled egg.

It sometimes happens that the cock will not leave the hen alone when she starts to sit. If she is continually persecuted in this way, the cock must be separated from her. Even if the cock remains quiet during the incubation period he will still need watching when the hen appears with her chicks. He may peck at them, and, if so, he must be removed. In any case, it is really better to remove him once the chicks are out. At 4 weeks old they may be considered independent and must be parted from their parents and allowed to lead their own life. The cock can then rejoin his mate and they will soon have a further nest.

For the first week the rearing food should consist of hard-boiled egg, small ants' eggs, crushed maw seed and finely cut up lettuce. The egg food must never be left long, for it sours quickly and is then dangerous to the health of the birds. Ants' eggs which have been lying about for days must also be removed. Finely ground senegal millet can be given quite early on; boiled millet is also excellent. It must be remembered that the birds do not remove the husks from the seed and need to be supplied with finely ground egg shell, lime and grit. The grit enables the birds to break the husk and grind the kernels. Small mealworms are soon taken.

Owing to their nervous disposition, quail are very easily disturbed when nesting and for this reason cannot be considered very reliable breeders. Experiments have been made at hatching the eggs in a small incubator and then transferring the chicks to a foster-mother. To do this successfully, however, requires a great deal of experience and the beginner would be better advised to leave the eggs with the quail in the hope that she will prove to be a good mother.

These quail are more susceptible to damp than to cold, and are well able to winter in an unheated indoor aviary, but if the cock continues to chase the hen and she shows signs of wishing to breed, it is better to part them and re-unite them in the spring. Three broods a year are not exceptional.

**Common Quail** *Coturnix coturnix*
*Origin* Europe, Asia

7 in. *Cock:* Head warm buff with two dark brown lines from beak to nape and with prominent whitish eyebrow stripes and short, dark moustache marks; cheeks warm brown, throat pale buff, both outlined with dark brown stripe from ear coverts, meeting under chin where it forms a black patch. Upper parts dark brown striated with buff and faintly mottled with black; breast and flanks reddish-brown flecked with black or dark brown and striated on flanks with prominent whitish marks; belly white or very pale buff. Tail brown, very short and almost completely concealed by the hairlike feathers of the rump. Beak and legs pale yellow; eye dark brown. *Hen:* Slightly larger than cock; less distinctly marked and lacking the dark band and patch on throat.

These small game birds are hardy and easy to keep although they nearly always remain wild and restless and are always inclined to fly straight up against the wire covering the aviary with resulting damage to their heads.

They nest readily if provided with ample cover in the form of low growing shrubs and coarse grass, the nest being a mere scrape in the centre of a grass tussock. Food consists of small seeds such as millet, broken wheat and groats, weed seeds, green stuff and insects. Ant cocoons are particularly welcome especially to the chicks, and for these canary rearing food or a fine grade insectivorous mixture should also be supplied. Grit is essential at all times and a sand bath should be provided in a dry and sheltered corner of the aviary.

All quail suffer from damp conditions and the aviary should therefore be well drained or a part of the flight should be roofed over.

**Rain Quail** *Coturnix coromandelica*
*Origin* India.

6 in. *Cock:* Resembles Common

Quail but black markings at the throat and neck are clearer; there is a large black spot in the centre of breast, sides of head are black with white margins. Wings brown, eyes brown, bill horn-coloured, legs flesh-coloured. *Hen* has no spot on breast and no black markings on white throat.

Rain Quail are imported irregularly but are offered at moderate prices. They are only very little larger than the Chinese Painted Quail *Excalfactoria chinensis* and a pair may well be kept with other birds in an aviary.

If during the first few days they are nervous and fly straight up, this will soon cease and they will become so tame that they will take mealworms from the hand. Like partridges, the hens grow tame very rapidly, the cocks are always a little more reserved. Exactly the opposite is the case with pheasants, where the cocks are always tamer than the hens.

To provide suitable conditions for the quail, give them a box of damp sharp river sand in which they can bathe. The ordinary sand which is on the market, and which is very good for some foreign birds, is not suitable for quail.

They will eat all manner of seeds, millet, maw, canary seed, rape seed and also insectivorous food (although personally I have seldom seen them touch it), and much green food, for preference chickweed and lettuce. All kinds of insects, flies, earwigs, earthworms, and mealworms are to their liking. The cock will carry every delicacy to the hen with the greatest care. In the evening they will huddle comfortably together and will usually roost in the sand box.

Breeding results are generally obtained in a small outside aviary. This must have the greater part covered with river sand, and partly covered with a fairly dense undergrowth so that a secluded nesting place can be found. The hen will lay her 10-12 eggs in a small hollow, lined with some fine grasses, and hatch them in 17 days.

If the cock should disturb the youngsters and peck at them (this happens occasionally when the mating instinct becomes too strong), he must be removed.

As a rule, however, everything goes quite well and the hen and cock may be seen tripping through the aviary with their family, all hunting for food, which should be strewn around on the ground during the first few days and later placed in the food bowls. Fine rearing food, which is used for canaries, is very suitable, also a little maw seed, and finely cut up lettuce or chickweed. Ants' eggs are not essential, but are greatly appreciated. If mealworms are cut up during the first few days small quantities of these can also be fed to the young.

The eggs may be hatched in an incubator and this is better than under a bantam hen, who is really rather large for these tiny youngsters and is apt to tread on them, with fatal results. They do very well in a brooder.

The birds may stay in the outside aviary during summer and winter providing an adjoining shelter is available and the temperature does not fall more than 10° below freezing point. On really cold frosty nights they must be accommodated in a frost-proof room.

**Harlequin Quail** *Coturnix delegorguei*
*Origin* South Africa.

6 in. *Cock:* Crown black-brown with a lighter centre stripe. A black stripe runs through eye extending behind ear

coverts. A white stripe runs above eye to nape. Cheeks and throat white, with a black band across cheeks, which continues down front and encircles throat. The breast is black in the centre with red-brown stripes running lengthways to the sides. Belly and under tail coverts brown-red. Upper parts black-brown with small lighter cross stripes and with long yellow stripes over the scapulars and back. Bill light horn-coloured, eye light brown, legs light yellow-brown. *Hen:* Black, as well as white, markings on head and throat entirely absent or only very lightly indicated. Throat whitish, the remainder of the under parts brown with light margins and paler black markings.

This species has become common in Europe and large numbers are bred annually.

The treatment of this quail should be exactly the same as that given to the Chinese Painted Quail. The hen produces 2 clutches in a season, each containing up to 10 eggs, which are laid in a slight hollow in the ground. Incubation lasts 17 days and if the hen will not sit, an incubator may be used with every confidence. At 4 weeks the young resemble the adult and their sex is apparent. When the old hen starts laying again, the youngsters must be removed.

Although one pair of quail may be kept with another pair of related quail for some months before the breeding season, this procedure becomes risky the moment a hen starts to lay. The cocks will suddenly start a murderous fight and, before intervention is possible, one of the fighters may be scalped.

But the Harlequin Quail is ideal to keep with other birds, since it keeps on the ground and never interferes with those on the perches. They will eat all the spilt seed scattered from the food trays and are usually tame and confiding.

**Button Quail** (African Bustard Quail)
*Turnix lepurana*
*Origin* Southern half of Africa.

*Hen* 6 in. *Cock* 5 in. *Cock:* Upper parts yellow-brown with light margins to the feathering of mantle. Crown of head is alternately barred with pale yellow and dark brown. Back and sides are spotted with black. Chin and throat are duller in colour and have fewer markings. *Hen:* Upper parts rusty-brown, with a reddish-yellow stripe over the crown; a similar stripe runs above eyes. Sides of head brownish. Feathers of mantle and scapulars show black cross banding and yellow margins. Throat and chin white with a transverse stripe of rust colour running across the crop and breast. Sides are brown-yellow with black drop-like markings, the under parts being whitish. Eyes yellow, bill grey-blue, legs flesh-coloured. It is a remarkable fact that the hen of this species is larger and more colourful than the cock.

In the family life of these birds the hens play a leading role. The call note, which resembles a deep powerful grumble, is produced by the hen and it is she also who is inclined to peck at the head of her mate. This is apt to play havoc with the beauty of the much more delicately-built cock. It is therefore imperative that the small aviary necessary for such a pair has dense planting in which the cock can retreat to safety. Yet several hens kept together usually live in complete harmony. They walk very carefully, lifting their feet high at each step. The cock will seek out a nesting-place and will scratch a hole in the ground. Nesting material is gathered from nearby; it consists of fine grasses and these will be deposited in the hollow. The cock, which usually does the hatching, will pull some grasses over himself and thus become practically invisible.

The hen will lay 6 to 8 eggs which are incubated by the cock for 13 days. For rearing the brood a diet of small ants' eggs, which should be mixed for preference with maw and egg food, is required. For the first few days the eyes of the youngsters do not entirely open, and look like pinheads. They will soon learn to pick the ants' eggs from the bill of the cock.

As a rule, the hen will play no part in the rearing of the youngsters; on the contrary, she sometimes starts chasing the cock away. When this happens, she must be separated and the cock left in peace to perform his task, which he does excellently, by himself.

Soon the youngsters learn to fend for themselves and start picking up ants' eggs; if care be taken that a fresh supply is always available for a further week, everything will go smoothly. After that time they will eat maw, egg food and cut up mealworms. They scarcely touch green food. Pieces of lime and germinated seed are readily taken.

After 6 weeks the youngsters will have grown to the same size as the parents and will resemble them in almost every detail. The young cocks, however, can be picked out straight away as they are appreciably smaller and duller in colour than the young hens.

At the early age of only 3 months, the hens are ready to breed and the pairs have to be sorted out and separated. The hens will be considerably tamer than the cocks.

It is a great pity that these quail are so little imported and that the price remains so high. An Australian species has been offered occasionally during the last few years, the Australian Button Quail (Rufous-chested Bustard Quail) *Turnix pyrrhothera*, which, though somewhat larger in size, needs the same treatment.

**Chukor Partridge** *Alectoris graeca chukar*
*Origin* India, Himalaya and Nepal.

14 in. *Cock:* Larger and more stocky than hen, with a fiery red bill. Colour, beige-grey with a yellowish white throat and fore neck, surrounded by a band of black. On the sides there are black bars on a brown-yellow ground. Legs, with small spurs, red and a red orbital ring. *Hen:* is distinctly smaller than cock and normally lacks spurs, although some older hens occasionally develop small spurs.

A primary condition for the keeping of these partridges is a roomy aviary, in which a rockery can be constructed, for it is on rocky ground amongst stones and boulders that these active birds feel most at home. They will become tame very readily, especially the hen; it may even be found possible to give her the run of the garden. Only one hen can be run with each cock; should more be introduced he will select one and almost certainly kill the others.

During breeding season a pair should be separated and placed in a well-planted aviary, where the hen is able to find refuge from the too-pressing attentions of her tempestuous mate. Some 8–12 eggs are laid in a shallow depression, usually hidden behind stones, in early May. If the hen then seems unwilling to start incubation, the eggs may be put under a broody bantam hen or in an incubator. After 24 days the youngsters will appear. They should be fed during the first few days with finely cut-up green food, lettuce and chickweed, maw seed and egg food. Later on some millet can be offered. It will be quite 3 months before the young birds assume the full adult plumage. The bill, which is black at first, then begins to turn red. The cocks are usually distinguishable by their deportment, but it is only after 8 months that the spurs become visible. If the eggs are regularly removed each day, the hen will continue to lay until she has produced as many as 40 in a season.

Outside of the breeding season these partridges may be given the liberty of the garden, providing their wings have been slightly clipped or they have been permanently pinioned by a veterinary surgeon.

In theory it should be safe to keep them with any other species in a large aviary and although they never chase or attempt to harm perching birds, in my own case a cock Chukor killed all my young Chinese Painted Quail. It would therefore appear to be unwise to associate them with any other ground birds.

These partridges may be kept outside, summer and winter. In order to keep them in good condition it is essential to maintain an adequate supply of green food; this seems to be preferred even to insect food.

**Red-legged Partridge** *Alectoris rufa rufa* Pl. 3
*Origin* Parts of Central and Southern Europe. Introduced to Britain in 1770 and now well established.

About 14 in. *Cock:* Forecrown grey, crown and hind neck rufous; broad whitish eyebrow streak extending onto nape; chin and throat white bordered with black, the black running through eyes, lores, and over beak. Upper breast warm buff flecked with black; breast blue-grey; abdomen cinnamon; flanks grey broadly barred with white, black, and chestnut. Whole of upper parts olive-brown. Iris red-brown, orbital ring red; bill, legs and feet red. *Hen:* Slightly smaller and duller, and lacks spur-like knobs which are carried by adult cocks.

In a large aviary with plenty of tall, rough grass and low shrubs these partridges will do well on a grain mixture, green food and a few live insects daily. The cocks like to stand on a raised hummock or tree stump to call and a log or even a large rock placed in the aviary will be appreciated. They will make a slovenly nest of grass in a shallow scrape, concealed in tall grass, and 12–18 brownish-yellow eggs, spotted and blotched with purple and brown will be laid. Incubation lasts about 24 days and the young may be reared as described for the Chukor Partridge. Red-legged Partridges are not good mixers with their own kind, and only one pair should be kept in an aviary. They are completely hardy and may be kept in the aviary summer and winter.

**Golden Pheasant** *Chrysolophus pictus* Pl. 20
*Origin* Northwest China.
*Cock* 40–44 in. *Hen* 25½–27 in. *Cock:* On crown of head is a crest of elongated, silky, bright golden-yellow feathers. Ear-band is a brownish grey, other parts of the face, chin, throat and neck are brownish red. The tippet or

ruff is formed of broad, rectangular feathers, the visible part of which is light orange in colour. Every feather in the tippet has two dark-blue bars across the tip. Upper part of back is deep green, and every feather is margined with velvet black. Lower part of back and rump are of a deep golden-yellow colour. Tail feathers are mottled and predominantly black and brown. Wings feature the colours dark red on the wing-tips; deep blue tertiaries; black and brown bands on primary and secondary quills. Entire under part of the bird is scarlet, merging into a light chestnut in the middle of the abdomen and the thigh parts. Under-tail coverts are red. The iris and the naked skin round the eye are light yellow; the bill and legs are a horn-yellow. *Hen:* Plumage of hen is much plainer than that of cock. The colours are mainly light, medium and a very dark brown, with an occasional pale-yellow feather. The feathers show a black mottled or barred design. It should be noted in passing that among the hens variations in the intensity of colour do occur.

Iris is brown, skin round the eyes is yellow, bill and legs are a horn-yellow. Information given concerning Lady Amherst's Pheasant also holds good for the Golden Pheasant. The two species closely resemble each other in characteristics. The incubation period of the Golden is, however, one day shorter – 23 days. Care and treatment is little trouble and should be the same as for the other pheasants.

**Lady Amherst's Pheasant** *Chrysolophus amherstiae* Pl. 19
*Origin* Tibet and Burma.
    *Cock* 52–68 in. *Hen* 26–27 in. *Cock:* Crown covered with short metallic-

green feathers; narrow crest of stiff, elongated crimson feathers; ruff of rounded feathers, white with a blue-and-black border; mantle and scapulars of scale-like feathers, metallic bluish-green with a black border edged with scintillant green; feathers of back broad and square, black with a green bar and a wide, buff-yellow fringe; those of rump with a vermilion fringe; tail coverts mottled black and white with long orange-vermilion tips; central rectrices irregularly lined black and white with black cross-bars; other rectrices similar on the narrow inner web, silver-grey passing to brown on the outer webs, with curved black bars; wings dark metallic blue with black borders, the primaries only blackish brown sparsely barred with buff; face and throat black, with metallic-green spots, breast-like mantle, borders of feathers wider and brighter; rest of under parts pure white, the base of the feathers grey, except the lower flanks and vent, which are barred with black and brown; under-tail coverts black and dark green more or less barred with white. Iris pale yellow; bare facial skin and lappet bluish or greenish white; bill and feet bluish grey. *Hen:* Similar to Golden Pheasant hen, but larger, the dark barring blacker, with a green sheen; sides of head, neck, mantle, lower throat and upper breast strongly washed with reddish chestnut; upper throat and abdomen pale, sometimes white; lores, cheeks and ear coverts silvery grey spotted with black; back strongly vermiculated; tail feathers rounded, not pointed at the tip, as in Golden Pheasants, and much more strongly marked with broad irregular bars of black, buff and pale grey vermiculated with black. Iris brown, sometimes pale yellow or greyish in older birds; orbital skin light slaty blue; bill and legs bluish grey.

This Pheasant has been known in Britain since 1828, and on the Continent of Europe since a little later than that. Owing to a great shortage of hens in the early days of their introduction, they were frequently crossed with hen Golden Pheasants. The resulting young proved fertile, but at the same time resulted in the loss of the pure racial qualities of this Pheasant.

In several countries breeders have now built up strains of pure bred birds and any fancier who intends to keep this species should make every effort to obtain pure bred stock. Any signs of red feathers intermixed with the white on the breast of the cock birds is a certain indication that there is Golden blood in its ancestry. The hens are more difficult to distinguish but generally speaking the Golden hen shows a more yellowish tone of body feathers and has yellow legs. The Amherst hen is greyish brown and her legs are grey. Hybrid hens nearly always have yellowish legs and such birds should be avoided.

Like the Goldens, these Pheasants have acclimatized themselves perfectly. They may be kept outside in summer and winter, but it is imperative to have a good shelter available.

Some seem to prefer roosting outside even when the snow falls. They can be prevented from doing so by removing the roosting perches from the flight and leaving only a platform with a thick layer of straw in the shelter. The Pheasants will then roost there; their legs will be in the straw and at the same time their bellies will be well protected from the cold.

Incubation takes 24 days. Two or even three hens may be run with one cock. As a rule, the hens will sit well and will rear their brood admirably. But many fanciers prefer to place the eggs under a bantam hen or in an incubator and to let the pheasant hatch and raise only the second clutch of the season.

The display of the cock during the mating time is most interesting to watch. The collar is spread and drawn to one side, and the gorgeous colours of the mantle are then revealed in all their beauty.

**Elliot's Pheasant** *Syrmaticus ellioti*
**Origin** Southeast China.

*Cock* 32 in. *Hen* 20 in. *Cock:* Bright red orbital patch, greenish beak. Crown and sides of head light grey with dark brown shading. White eyebrow stripe, a row of little white feathers with black tips under the eye. Back and breast bright copper with black markings and a metallic sheen. Wings chestnut-brown and blue-black with white bands. Tail grey and brown, margined with black. Legs green-grey. *Hen:* Has a beige-red head with a red-brown crown. Pale grey feathers under the eyes. Neck grey to black with white margins, to the small feathers. White belly, brown-grey tail with narrow dark barring and black-and-white spots.

The demand for pheasants is increasing and the Elliot's is being kept more and more. Small wonder, since his exquisite colouring is astounding. It is imperative that a large aviary be available with thick planting and high roosting perches if a cock and a couple of hens are to be kept in good health and condition. It is even more desirable to keep the cock by himself in a centre aviary and his ladies in adjoining aviaries. The cock is very fierce and continually chases the hens, which become completely exhausted and are sometimes dangerously wounded. If desired some hen Golden or Common Game Pheasants may be put in with the cock for company, but it is most probable that he will not even look at them.

A 3 ft high shield of matting should be fixed between the aviaries. The cock can then be placed with one hen on one day and another hen the next day, and then set apart again. In this way the hens get some peace and at the same time it is reasonably certain that their eggs will be fertilized.

An Elliot's hen will usually start to lay in March, one egg every other day. As she will lay about 20 eggs in a season they must be collected regularly and placed in an incubator or, better still, under a bantam hen which can run with the youngsters when they hatch. A 3-year-old pheasant hen, however, may usually be relied upon to hatch and rear her own chicks and may be allowed to keep the last eight eggs which she lays.

Incubation takes 25 days. The method of rearing young Elliot's Pheasants is similar to that described for other species. With rearing food or finely ground egg food and rusks and bread, ants' eggs and finely cut up meal-worms should be given. If this is done, all will go well. Plenty of chopped green food, lettuce for preference, should also be supplied. Drinking water in shallow dishes must always be available.

It is only after about 10 weeks, when the adult plumage begins to show, that the young cocks can be recognized by their grey-yellow tail quills.

The youngsters will attain full colouring the same year – which is a great advantage to the breeder if he wishes to dispose of surplus stock as colourful birds always find a ready market. In contrast, the Lady Amherst's and other Pheasants must be kept for about 2 years before they are in full colour and will fetch a good price.

If young birds are being bought, the parents should be inspected as there is such a diversity in types and a start made with mediocre birds from poor stock will never produce satisfactory results.

If eggs are purchased to be hatched in an incubator the fancier from whom they are obtained should have a reputation for keeping good stock.

## Hume's Bar-tailed Pheasant

*Syrmaticus humiae humiae* Pl. 18.
*Origin* Manipur, the Lushai and the Chin Hills.

*Cock* 32 in. *Hen* 20 in. *Cock:* Crown brown; neck, upper mantle, chin and throat metallic steel-blue; mantle fiery-red; lower back and rump blue-green with narrow white fringe; wings fiery bronze-red with small sub-terminal black spots, shoulder stripe and two bars on secondaries white; breast chestnut with bluish gloss and fiery margins; belly and sides chestnut; middle tail feathers greyish-white with narrow bars of chestnut and black; outer feathers mainly black with grey bars. Bare facial patch crimson, beak horn-coloured, legs and feet black. *Hen:* Very similar to Elliot's hen but without black on throat and fore neck.

This pheasant is very similar to Elliot's Pheasant to which it is closely related. It is rare in captivity but its treatment should be as for the other Long-tailed Pheasants of the same genus.

Chicks when first hatched are very

small and require special care during
the early stages of rearing. For the first
few days they do not readily accept
food unless it is 'moving' and should
therefore be given a liberal supply of
insects. Once they have passed this
stage however they usually progress
normally on the treatment and food
supplied to other species of pheasant
chicks.

**Mikado Pheasant** *Syrmaticus mikado*
Pl. 17.
*Origin* Mount Arizan, Central Formosa.
*Cock* 35 in. *Hen* 21.2 in. *Cock:* Predominantly black, feathers of the head,
back and lower breast laced with steel-
blue and those of the throat, neck and
upper breast having a violet-purple
lustre. Coverts and flights black with
triangular white marks on the former.
Tail black, central feathers much
prolonged and all barred with white.
Facial patch bright crimson, beak and
feet black. *Hen:* Dark brown heavily
mottled, ligher on throat and upper
breast. Tail shorter than male, central
feathers bright chestnut with buff and
black transverse bars. Facial patch
smaller and paler in colour. Beak, legs
and feet brownish-black.

Feeding and treatment as for Elliot's
Pheasant, but they require large
quantities of green food at all times.
They are hardy but dislike damp,
foggy winter weather and should be
kept on very well drained soil.

**Reeves's Pheasant** *Syrmaticus reevesi*
*Origin* Central China. Pl. 16.
*Cock* 84 in. *Hen* 30 in. *Cock:* Head,
chin, throat and nape white margined
below with a black collar and with a
broad black line from beak passing
through the eye and meeting behind
the head. Mantle, back and rump
golden-buff, wing coverts white all

margined with black. Breast and sides
of body white barred and margined
with chestnut, flanks white margined
with buff and remainder of under parts
black. Tail up to 5 ft in length, two
central feathers silvery barred with
chestnut and black and remainder
cinnamon barred with black. *Hen:*
Head brown with yellowish-buff on
sides of face, ear coverts and nucal
band blackish. Mantle chestnut tipped
with grey and mottled with black.
Body and wing coverts are mainly
greyish-brown with white, buff and
black markings. Long tail is pointed
and greyish-brown barred with buff
and black and with black and white
tips to the feathers. Breast and abdomen is lighter in tone, shading from
chestnut to buff lightly mottled. The
beauty of these Pheasants is only seen
to advantage if they are kept in a very
large aviary. The tail, almost 6 ft long,
needs special attention. The roosting
perches must be placed so high up and
so far away from the walls that the tail
cannot be damaged when the bird flies
up. The cock should be given at least
two or even three hens for mating. The
care needed is similar to that given to
other pheasants. Reeves's Pheasants
are one of the hardiest species and may
be kept outside during summer and
winter. It is, however, always preferable to remove the perches from the
open flight during the winter and to
provide a platform with a good layer
of straw in the shelter on which the
birds will roost.

It may happen that the cock is too
fierce, and this may spell danger for the
hens. If so, he must be kept in a
separate pen and only allowed with the
hens until mating has taken place.
After this he must be again removed.
Usually the hens will sit well, but many

people prefer to entrust the eggs to a bantam hen or to place them in an incubator. If fertile, they hatch in 24 days.

The rearing of the young should be similar to that of other species already described; if possible give plenty of green food and mealworms and it is vital to keep the youngsters dry.

**Black-breasted Kalij** (Horsfield's Kalij) *Lophura leucomelana lathami* Pl. 10
*Origin* Eastern Bhutan, Assam and Upper Burma.

*Cock* 23 in. *Hen* 20 in. *Cock:* Entire plumage black, glossed with purple, the feathers of the lower back, rump and upper tail coverts margined with white. Crest long and the feathers hair-like. Facial wattles deep scarlet. Legs and feet and also beak blue-black. *Hen:* Olive-brown, chin and throat whitish; wings and ventral feathers tipped with buff. Central tail feathers shorter than those of male and of a deep ferruginous tone.

Feeding and treatment as for Silver Pheasant.

**Silver Pheasant** *Lophura n. nycthemera* Pl. 11
*Origin* South China.

*Cock* 48–50 in. *Hen* 28 in. *Cock:* This pheasant is the largest and whitest of all Silver Pheasants of which there are many sub-species. Upper body has a chalk-white colour with three to four narrow black lines running across each feather in a wavy pattern. Under parts, the chin, the throat and the long crest are a magnificent, glossy, deep bluish-black. The rectrices are very striking because of their great length. The central pair is pure white and the remainder are decorated on the outer web by a few narrow broken black lines.

The cock Silver Pheasant assumes the adult plumage only in the second

year. The immature dress is considerably different from the full dress; it does not have the pure white upper-body, but is finely vermiculated white, reddish-yellow and black. The tail has not yet attained its full length and resembles the tail of the hen, though longer and more coarsely vermiculated. Crest and under parts dull black. V-shaped white lines are running across under parts. *Hen:* Though the hens show a great deal of individual variation, it may safely be said that they are mainly olive-brown with more or less inconspicuous black vermiculation. Chin and throat are spotted with grey and crest is tipped with black.

This pheasant is a closer relative of our domestic poultry than the other species already described, and may have chickens as companions in the aviary or be allowed to run free in the garden. For food it will be quite content with mash and grain as supplied to the chickens.

Breeding and hatching usually presents no difficulty; the hen will sit steadily for 25 or 26 days on as many as 15 eggs and will rear her young admirably.

Normal rearing food and special chick grain should be made available, but, most important of all, the young must be guarded against damp and cold.

Only during the second year will the birds begin to show colour; the hens will lay a very few eggs during the first year but in the second year up to 16 eggs may be expected. The birds are very tolerant but are not to be trusted in an aviary with small finches which are breeding as they will almost certainly devour any youngsters which have just left the nest.

These birds are much quieter than

other pheasants and every fancier who keeps chickens might well run a few with them. It should, however, be mentioned that the cocks can be exceedingly savage towards any intruder when the hens are laying and they will not hesitate to attack their owner with beak and spurs, sometimes inflicting quite a painful wound.

## The Imperial Pheasant *Lophura imperialis*

*Cock* 30 in. *Hen* 24 in. *Cock:* Colour of entire body dark steel-blue. Body feathers black with a broad blue fringe. Those of the lower back and rump, wing and tail coverts deep black with bright metallic-blue borders. The pure black crest is rather short and pointed. The long broad and slightly arched central rectrices are pointed and have brown spots, as well as back and wings. Skin of face or wattle scarlet, legs crimson. Eyes a reddish-orange and bill a pale yellowish-green, base blackish. The cocks assume adult plumage at the age of eighteen months. *Hen:* Feathers of crown are somewhat elongated and often raised but do not form a real crest. Head is light greyish-brown, cheeks, chin and throat paler. Upper parts are chestnut with inconspicuous black spots, under parts are light greyish-brown and sometimes slightly mottled.

## Edwards' Pheasant *Lophura edwardsi*
Pl. 12
*Origin* Northern border of Quang-Tri, Annam.

*Cock* 23–26 in. *Hen* 16 in. *Cock:* Tail is rather short, compared with the other dimensions of the body. It is quite straight except for the two central rectrices, which are somewhat rounded and blunt-ended. The crest is generally white, lightly flecked with black, and it is quite short. The overall colour of the body is dark blue with broad metallic blue edges to the feathers. On the lower back, tail coverts and rump, these edges are preceded by a deep velvet-black border. The outer fringe of the wing coverts has a more greenish tone. Bill is greenish white, tarsi are crimson, iris is reddish brown. Face-wattles are scarlet and can be distended into two large, scarlet lobes. *Hen:* As most other pheasant hens, the hen Edwards' is mainly brown, though in this case the brown tends to chestnut. This colour is richest on the mantle, and dullest – almost brown-grey – on the head and the neck. There is hardly any crest. Entire plumage is covered by almost invisible black vermiculations. The six central rectrices are dark brown, others black. The same division of colour can be seen on the primaries. The bill is a horny brown, face and legs scarlet and the eyes brown.

## Swinhoe's Pheasant *Lophura swinhoei*
Pl 13
*Origin* Mountain forests of Formosa.

*Cock* 30–32 in. *Hen* 21 in. *Cock:* The chief characteristic of this pheasant is its crest, which is mainly white but has a few black streaks, similar to the crest of Edwards' Pheasant. With the exception of an irregularly shaped white patch on back, its head, neck, back and under parts are a glossy blue. One recognizes the same pattern of cross-bars that is found with Edwards' Pheasant on the feathers of rump, lower back and tail-coverts. The Swinhoe's pattern is different from the Edwards' as the black subterminal bar is narrower and the blue border is wider. The wing-coverts are black with green borders; the scapulars are red, and together with the white patch on the back they are the typical characteristics of the Swinhoe's.

Tail is dark blue apart from the two greatly elongated central rectrices, which are entirely white and pointed. Bill is horn-yellow, legs crimson, iris reddish-brown and face-wattles are scarlet. *Hen:* Face and the throat are dull white to pale grey. Body feathers are mainly chestnut vermiculated black. On the breast the black vermiculation is in a V-shaped pattern, fading into abdomen.

Bill is horn-yellow, legs are crimson, eyes brown. Young cocks have an immature plumage in their first year; not until the second do they have their full dress and reach maturity.

These birds are very hardy and may remain outside during summer and winter if the run is well drained and kept dry. A shelter must, of course, be available. The cock is apt to be fierce during the mating time, so the aviary should be roomy and well planted, in order to give the hens a chance to seek cover. A careful watch must be kept for the cock may chase them so much that they become distressed and severely wounded. Should this occur, the cock must be removed.

As a rule, Swinhoe's Pheasants are excellent breeders and rear their young well. The eggs, may, however, be hatched in an incubator or under a bantam hen.

The greatest care must be taken with artificial rearing to keep the young dry, for damp and cold are very bad for them and give rise to digestive troubles which usually end fatally. A good pheasant rearing food is now on the market.

# Junglefowl

Four species of Junglefowl are known, distributed over eastern and southern India, Burma and Malaysia to Java. They live in the forests and thickets but usually come into the open to feed, often on roadsides or into the cultivated fields near villages, in the early morning and evening. Their food consists of seeds, berries and insects and in captivity a diet similar to that provided for other pheasants is suitable.

They are polygamous and each cock should be provided with two or more hens. Usually they prove to be good and prolific breeders and if provided with a good sized enclosure with plenty of natural cover, the hens will incubate and rear their own chicks. Often however it is more convenient to use bantams as foster parents. Incubation takes from 18 to 21 days and the chicks are inclined to prove delicate when first hatched. They should therefore be kept from damp and cold until they are well grown and given the same treatment as the most delicate pheasant chicks.

Adult Junglefowl are powerful fliers and it is not safe to attempt to keep them at liberty in a garden unless they are pinioned but in a large park it is possible to establish them full winged. In an aviary never more than once cock should be kept as they are extremely aggressive towards their own kind and fighting, which is certain to occur if two cocks meet, is usually fatal.

They are delightful birds to keep and although imported specimens are usually shy and retiring, birds bred in captivity often become very tame and will readily feed from the hand. Unfortunately however the voice of the cocks is shrill and loud and they crow at the break of dawn and often at intervals throughout the night. It is not therefore advisable to keep them in a built-up area where they are likely to prove disturbing to neighbours.

**Red Junglefowl** *Gallus gallus* Pl. 9
*Origin* Himalaya and East India, Burma, South China, Indo-China, Siam, Malay, Sumatra and Java and elsewhere in the Far East where it has been introduced and become naturalized.

Slightly larger than the domestic Old English Game Bantam. *Cock* 24 in. *Hen* much smaller. *Cock:* Head, neck and hackles reddish golden-brown, becoming straw-coloured on the longer hackles; mantle and coverts metallic green and purple; median coverts, scapulars and mantle dark maroon, rump orange-red. Flights cinnamon; tail metallic green. Under parts velvety-black. Face, high serrated comb and thoat wattles crimson with a white wattle below the ear. Beak, legs and feet blackish, legs furnished with long and exceedingly sharp spurs. *Hen:* Head rusty-red, neck and mantle orange shading to pale yellow, mottled with black; remainder of upper parts dull brown finely mottled with black. Throat, foreneck chestnut; remainder of under parts pale, light red. Very small comb, face and small throat wattles as cock.

This is by far the most hardy of the Junglefowl and is of particular interest as being the wild ancestor of all the many breeds of domestic poultry. Birds reared in captivity are usually available but unfortunately it has been freely crossed with domestic Game bantams and stock should only be purchased which is bred from guaranteed pure parents. Yellow legs are usually an indication of impurity.

**Sonnerat's Junglefowl** (Grey Junglefowl) *Gallus sonnerati* Pl. 8
*Origin* Western, central and southern India.

*Cock* 29½ in. *Hen* 15 in. *Cock:* Hackles and mantle pencilled with grey, white and black, the tips of the feathers having the barbs united, forming yellowish-white spots which have the appearance of sealing-wax. Wing coverts orange-red with the same peculiar formation. Back, lesser coverts and under parts dark brown or blackish, the feathers having a fringe and central stripe of grey. Rump and tail coverts purplish, tail feathers metallic green. Serrated comb and wattles crimson. Beak and legs yellow, the latter with a tinge of red. *Hen:* Mantle rusty-brown with broad buff shaft marks; upper parts brown mottled with black and with light shaft marks. Under parts mainly white, fringed and lightly mottled with black and with a wash of brown on the abdomen.

This species is reasonably hardy but should be provided with a frost-proof shelter in winter and in excessively cold weather it would be as well to arrange for some form of artificial heating, as the birds are of a rather sluggish nature. The chicks are delicate and slow growing and need special care during the early stages of rearing. As with all species of Junglefowl, the cocks can be exceedingly spiteful.

**The Firebacks**
The Firebacks, which owe their name to a bright red patch on the lower back and rump, are divided into two groups, dependent on whether they are crested or crestless.

The Crestless Firebacks are very rare. Practically nothing is known about their habits and few specimens have ever been introduced into Europe.

The Crested Firebacks are more common in pheasantries and more is also known about their life in the wild state. After the last war a few were shipped to Europe, and although at present birds of this species are rare, in time they should be more generally found. They live wild in Siam, Cochin China, Malaya, Sumatra, Banka and Borneo.

Both sexes have a short, thick crest of crowded stiff feathers. In the hens the crest is much less developed than in the cocks.

### Bornean Crested Fireback Pheasant
*Lophura ignita ignita* Pl. 14
*Origin* Borneo, introduced into the Island of Banka.
*Cock* about 26 in. *Hen* 22 in.
*Cock:* General colour black with rich purple-blue sheen. Back, rump, belly and sides fiery bronze-red. Central tail feathers rich buff. Long bare-shafted crest. Bare facial skin blue, legs and feet reddish. *Hen:* General colour of upper parts rich chestnut lightly mottled with black; neck pale chestnut, chin and throat white; breast chestnut, remainder of under parts dark brown, all feathers edged with white. Facial skin, legs and feet as cock.

These pheasants cannot stand frost nor frequent wet, cold winter weather and consequently should be well sheltered during the winter months. The hens are inclined to lay late in the year and the chicks therefore need special care although they generally grow quickly under suitable conditions. They are however very subject to attack by various germs and their run must be kept scrupulously clean and placed on well drained soil.

### Siamese Fireback *Lophura diardi* Pl. 15
*Origin* Southern Shan States, Siam, Cambodia and Cochin China.
*Cock* 32 in. *Hen* 24 in. *Cock:* Head and throat black, long tufted crest steel-blue. Neck, mantle, breast and wings grey, finely vermiculated with black. Wing coverts with white edges and a black band near tips. Upper back shining gold, lower back and rump bronzy-red. Under parts and tail black with steel-blue gloss. Face and legs scarlet, beak yellowish. *Hen:* Head and neck brown, mantle, outer tail feathers and under parts chestnut, lower breast and belly margined with white. Wings, central tail feathers, lower back and rump black mottled and banded with white. Face, beak and legs as male.

Siamese Firebacks are much easier to keep as aviary birds than any other of the Firebacks. They are far less susceptible to cold and frost, and when properly acclimatized they are hardy even in our inclement climate. Damp and snow are bad for them, however, and it is therefore better to confine them to the shelter if the weather is severe. As they are a hardy species, it is not necessary to heat their night shelter; but it is advisable to cover the floor with a thick layer of straw so as to prevent damage to the feet by frost. They are monogamous, but care should be taken during the mating season, as the male is apt to become too persistent in his advances and as adult cocks carry long and sharp spurs they may inflict serious injury to the hens.

### Japanese Green Pheasant (Southern Green Pheasant) *Phasianus versicolor versicolor* Pl. 6
*Origin* Japan except the island of Yezo.
Slightly smaller than the common Game Pheasant.

*Cock:* Crown, nape, mantle, throat, breast and belly dark metallic green; neck rich purple; scapulars coppery-red with the mantle feathers black centred, with fine buff margins; wing coverts bluish-grey; rump and upper tail coverts greenish-grey; tail greenish-grey barred with black and fringed with purple. Bare facial patches crimson; short ear tufts metallic green; beak horn-yellow; legs and feet blackish. *Hen:* Of a general sandy-buff marked and barred with dark brown and black. Neck and mantle with a pinkish tone and the centre of the latter black, feathers tipped with metallic green; lores, chin and throat clear buff and with a patch below the eye white; tail pinkish-buff barred with black and pale buff.

This pheasant shares the restless and wary nature of all the game pheasants and is usually rather wild in an aviary. If suddenly disturbed it is inclined to fly straight upwards and may seriously damage its head against the wire. It is essential therefore to provide it with a large aviary thickly planted with shrubs to give adequate cover into which it can retire.

In addition to the usual grain mixture they appreciate quantities of fresh greenstuff and live insects. The hens are usually good brooders and look after their chicks well provided they can make their nesting scrape in a quiet and well sheltered corner where there is no risk of being disturbed.

## The Monals

The Monals are true mountain birds; they are found in the eastern part of Afghanistan, the Himalayan Range and the mountains of western China.

Three distinct species exist, but their close relationship is so obvious that there is no ground for a generic distinction between them. Hence modern nomenclature unites all three in the genus *Lophophorus*, and all other names still in use are considered as synonyms. The three species are:

Himalayan Monal *Lophophorus impeyanus* Pl. 7
Chinese Monal *Lophophorus lhuysi*
Sclater's Monal *Lophophorus sclateri*

The colours of the Monal are overwhelmingly beautiful, and the bird may be considered one of the most magnificent representatives of the pheasant family. The only birds equalling the multi-coloured, metallic reflections – blue, purple, green and red – of the plumage of the Monals are Humming-birds and Birds of Paradise.

The display of the cock Monal is aimed at showing his wealth of colour to the fullest advantage. It is interesting to note that at all times during the display ritual the cock keeps one wing lowered, hiding his legs and feet from the hen.

On account of their adaptation to high altitudes, they prove extremely susceptible to a variety of infections. Soil suitable for Monals must be of a special texture, and accommodation has to meet specific requirements. Rain does not bother these birds, but stagnant, damp or sour ground is bad for them.

Monals are best kept on a coarse, sandy soil. They need a roomy pen. An area of 150 square feet is the minimum in which to ensure satisfactory breeding results. It is also essential to plant dense cover in the aviary. The birds like to have plenty of cover, and this induces them to breed more readily. In our wet climate Monals should not be allowed to sleep out in the open. A shelter of approximately 6 ft by 6 ft with perches should be provided. It is often found that these birds prefer a broad board to perches for roosting.

**Himalayan Monal** (Impeyan Pheasant) *Lophophorus impeyanus* Pl. 7
*Origin* The Himalayas, from Afghanistan to Bhutan.

Cock 28–29 in. Hen slightly smaller. *Cock:* Head, throat and high racket-shaped crest metallic green. Nape and side neck reddish-copper, mantle golden-green. Wings purple and blue, lower back pure white, rump and upper tail coverts shining blue, under parts dull black, tail chestnut. Beak blackish, legs and feet dark brown. *Hen:* Upper parts mostly brown streaked and mottled with buff, rump brown with distinct buff bar. Under parts paler brown with prominent white shaft stripes. Throat and half-collar white, tail dark brown with reddish-brown bars. Beak, legs and feet dark brown. Both sexes have the small naked eye patches blue.

**White Eared Pheasant** *Crossoptilon c. crossoptilon*
*Origin* The mountains of northwestern Yunnan, western Szechuan, and southwestern Tibet.

Cock 36.8 in. Hen a little smaller. *Cock:* Crown, short, curled feathers black. Elongated ear-coverts, entire body plumage pure white, greyish on wing and tail coverts; flights brownish. Tail similar in form to other Eared Pheasants, having twenty feathers, dark brown, glossed with green and with purple at the tips. Wattles crimson, beak horn-coloured. Legs and feet red, with short spurs. *Hen:* Similar but slightly smaller and without spurs. Unfortunately this lovely pheasant is now extremely rare and very few are to be found in captivity. It is said to be rather more delicate than the other Eared Pheasants but should be given the same food and treatment.

**Brown Eared Pheasant** (Hoki)
*Crossoptilon mantchuricum*
*Origin* Extreme northwestern China.

Cock 40 in. Hen slightly smaller. *Cock:* Crown black, the feathers being short and curled. Elongated ear coverts white; neck black shading into brown on mantle; lower back and rump dull greyish-white; breast blackish-brown, remaining under parts lighter. Tail similar in form to that of the Blue-Eared Pheasants but having 22 feathers, mainly whitish, the tips only being brown, glossed with purple and blue. Wattles crimson, beak pale horn, legs and feet red with short spurs. *Hen:* Similar but smaller and without spurs.

These Pheasants, which are still very costly, may run about at liberty together with other nearly-related species, provided one wing has been slightly clipped, or the bird permanently pinioned. The latter operation should, however, be performed by a veterinary surgeon. They become exceedingly tame and are very hardy. Indeed, they seem to prefer cold to heat. They are tolerant of other pheasants and domestic poultry. They should be kept in pairs and their only fault is their habit of digging, which they perform with their beaks. This is apt to damage plants and even shrubs and can ruin a lawn.

Should they be kept in an aviary, this would need to be large as otherwise from sheer boredom they are apt to resort to feather-plucking.

Adequate shelter should be provided from sun and rain. The

youngsters become adult and attain full colouring at 5 months. While they are being reared, insects should be liberally supplied also mealworms, earthworms and ants' eggs. Grated raw meat can be of great service. Unfortunately the cocks often prove to be infertile.

## Blue Eared Pheasant *Crossoptilon auritum*

*Origin* Mountains of Kokonor Kansu, eastern Tibet and northwestern Szechuan, western China.

*Cock* 38½ in. *Hen* similar or slightly smaller. *Cock:* General colour slate-blue, short curled feathers of crown black. Ear coverts white and much elongated giving the appearance of long, tufted ears. Chin and throat white. The tail is comprised of 24 long and wide feathers, arched and fringed, black glossed with purple and the outer pairs having the basal three-quarters white. Wattles crimson, beak long, stout and curved, horn-coloured. Legs and feet red, short, stout spurs. *Hen:* Similar but slightly smaller and without spurs.

The apparent difference between the sexes is very slight but the adult cock may be recognized by his spurs and more forceful appearance. These pheasants were first bred in captivity as recently as 1932. As well as quantities of green food and insects, they like tubers, roots and grubs which they dig out of the soil with their strong curved beaks. They never scratch the soil with their feet, as do domestic poultry. In addition to their beautiful slate-blue colouring and striking white ear tufts, they have a broad arched tail of lace-like feathers.

The hen will sit well and successfully rear the chicks but many fanciers will, however, prefer to hatch by incubator. The rearing of the young presents no special difficulties. Rearing food should be given as for other pheasants. Mealworms and other insects are important. Some cod liver oil mixed in the food is beneficial. A small quantity of finely chopped raw meat each day is excellent. The birds should be kept in pairs, and need more space than the smaller varieties. They can stand cold better than heat, but a first essential is a dry run.

## The Tragopans

The Tragopans form a very distinct genus of pheasants, differing widely from all other genera of the pheasant family. Five species are recognized, viz:

Western Tragopan
*Tragopan melanocephalus*
Satyr Tragopan T. *satyra* Pl. 4
Blyth's Tragopan T. *blythi blythi*
Temminck's Tragopan
T. *temmincki* Pl. 5
Cabot's Tragopan T. *caboti*
and a sub-species of T. *blythi*, T. *blythi molesworthi*, The Tibetan or Molesworth's Tragopan.

The pattern of their plumage is so elaborate and the colouring so varied that it is almost impossible to convey, by words alone, an accurate description of each species, especially to those who are not already familiar with the general appearance of these pheasants. Suffice it to say that the body plumage is predominantly red with white or pearl-like markings outlined with grey, brown, black or blue, depending on the species. The cocks have bare facial patches of violet, blue, scarlet or orange; short crests of hair-like feathers, black or black and orange-red; two fleshy horns, and brilliantly coloured bib-like throat wattles or lappets which are inflated during the display. In repose these ornamentations may be almost invisible but at the climax of the display the horns reach a height of 2–2¾ in. and the throat wattles a length of 4–6 in. and a width of 2–3 in. This ornamentation is unique to the Tragopans and the horns give rise to the English name of 'Horned Pheasants' and the German 'Horn-fasanen'. Total length 24–27 in.

The area of distribution of the Tragopans extends from Kashmir in the west, across the Himalayas and Burma into central China, where they are found at great heights, varying between 3,000 and 12,000 feet. Their food consists of leaves, berries, seeds and insects.

In contrast to other pheasants, they are strong fliers, and consequently far less earth-bound. They frequently feed in trees and often adopt old nests made by crows or other large birds. If however there is no ready-made nest available, hen Tragopans will build a well constructed nest of branches and twigs, often at a quite considerable height above the ground. In an aviary therefore it is advisable to construct an artificial nest or nesting platform in a tall shrub or on suspended branches. A shallow fruit basket or large wicker tray will serve the purpose well and the presence of such an artificial nest may well encourage breeding.

Tragopans are perfectly hardy, and in fact require protection from summer heat more than from winter cold. Plenty of natural shade should therefore be provided. One disadvantage is that these birds do not survive long in small pens but if provided with large, well-planted enclosures they live to a ripe old age, and satisfactory breeding results may be expected.

In captivity their food should consist of the same mixture of seeds and grains as required for other pheasants, but it is absolutely essential to supply large quantities of fruit and greenstuffs daily, bearing in mind however that any kind of cabbage is bad for Tragopans. Insects of most kinds are greatly appreciated especially when young are being reared.

**Bornean Great Argus** *Argusianus argus grayi* Pl. 21
*Origin* Interior of Borneo.
*Cock* 68–80 in. *Hen* 29.6–30.4 in. *Cock:* Head and neck bare and blue in colour, apart from short black feathers on top of the head and nape. General colour above black mottled and dotted with buff and with white on mantle and coverts. Neck and upper breast rusty-red with lighter shaft marks. Secondaries and flights grey-brown with narrow wavy lines of black and dark brown, the former developed to an abnormal length and having the outer webs decorated with a row of large ocelli, yellow white and reddish in colour, each enclosed by a narrow margin of black. Central tail feathers very long and broad, tapering to narrow points, greyish-brown on inner webs and rufous on outer, finely vermiculated with black and buff. When fully developed these tail feathers may reach a length of 4 ft. Under parts rufous, finely mottled and barred with dark brown and black. Beak yellowish-horn, legs and feet red. *Hen:* Much like cock, but lacking the long wings and tail.

The Argus Pheasants are only very occasionally found in private collections as they are difficult to obtain and consequently are very expensive. There are three species distributed throughout the Malay Peninsula, Sumatra and Borneo, where they are found at low and moderate altitudes. The Bornean species is very distinct from those in the two other regions.

Only in display does the cock reveal his truly marvellous splendour. In repose he appears a rather drab bird. In a wild state the Argus are not rare, in contrast to the small numbers found in captivity but they are excessively wary and consequently are seldom seen. They prefer dry, rocky country, at heights from sea level to about 1,300 metres.

The hens fly strongly but the cocks are rather awkward in their flight due to the abnormal development of their secondary feathers.

It is known that the sexes live apart throughout the year. Only during the breeding season do the hens seek out a cock, but probably associate with him only for the brief period necessary for mating to take place. Argus cocks bred in captivity prove dangerous to the chicks and it is advisable to remove the former from the aviary as soon as it is certain that mating has taken place. The aviaries in which Argus are to be kept should, of course, be very spacious, because of the enormous length of the cock's tail and wing feathers.

The hen is usually an excellent mother and should be allowed to rear her own chicks. This will restrict her laying to a single clutch in a season, but it is preferable to have two live chicks rather than any amount of failures. Argus chicks grow slowly and have to be given a great deal of care during the first year. They should not be left without artificial heat during the first winter. They fully mature only in their third year, after which the wing and tail feathers continue to grow for another three to four years, before reaching their full length. Even fully adult Argus never really become accustomed to our damp winters and adequate protection at night is therefore essential. This species is relatively peaceable and does not resent the company of other species of pheasant but it is not advisable to attempt to keep two or more cock Argus together however large their aviary may be.

## Peafowl

The Peafowl are polygamous and in the wild state usually live in small groups of one cock with as many as five hens. The hens nest on the ground, usually in tall, thick grass or amongst dense shrubs, the clutch consisting of four to eight eggs. Incubation takes from 27 to 30 days, usually 28 days. The Peahen is a good mother, and the chicks are easy to rear, though they do not grow rapidly.

Their large size and the magnificent train of the cocks give the birds an imposing appearance. Their feeding is very simple, grain and greenstuffs are all they need although they will greedily eat insects and indeed a certain amount of animal food is essential to the young chicks. When at liberty in a large garden or park, however, they will find a large part of their food for themselves. Peafowl may be kept in pens, but they must have plenty of space if their plumage is to remain in good condition. They can safely be associated with other birds, even with pheasants, and when at liberty will often seek the company of domestic poultry.

The two main species, the Indian, *Parvo cristatus*, and the Burmese, *Parvo muticus*, cross freely, producing completely fertile hybrids.

**Indian or Blue Peafowl** *Parvo cristatus* Pl. 22, 23, 24.

This is the universally known, common bird that has been kept and reared outside its natural state so long that it has undergone a number of variations in size and build. Albinism occurred frequently and an entirely white variety is now well established. In the open country where the air is free from soot and other pollution and the plumage can be kept clean, this is a very beautiful variety and due to the peculiar structure of the feathers, the ocelli can be clearly seen, with the faint colouring and iridescence of mother-o'-pearl.

Pied Peafowl, resulting from a cross between the white and normal forms, are frequently seen and have areas of white of varying size, indiscriminately mixed with the normal colouring. Such birds are not particularly attractive and the cross is better avoided.

A further variety, the Black-winged Peafowl is, as its name implies, much darker in colouring, the wings of the cocks being almost entirely black. The hens, on the other hand, are much lighter in general colour than those of the true species and are often pied.

**Green Peafowl** (Burmese Peafowl) *Parvo muticus*
Origin: Southeastern Assam, Burma, Siam, Indo-China, Malay and Java, but, strangely enough, not in Sumatra nor in Borneo. They are even more beautiful in colouring than the Indian species, also their legs are longer and

the hens more closely resemble the cocks except that they lack the magnificent train. An unusual feature is that the hens also carry spurs on the tarsi, which in nearly all other species of gallinaceous birds is a characteristic of the male sex only.

Young cocks which have not developed their train can still be distinguished from hens fairly readily by the colouring of the bare facial patch which is brown in the hens but bluish-black in the cocks.

In their habits and feeding the Green Peafowl much resemble the Indian, though they are usually rather wilder and more wary. They do well in an aviary or at liberty in a park but they are less hardy and require some protection during the winter. They breed readily but the chicks are not so easily reared and must be protected from frost, especially at night when they are best shut in a closed pen. Provided this is well constructed of stout materials it should not be necessary to provide artificial heat.

The cocks, unfortunately, are exceedingly aggressive and it is not possible to keep them together, even at liberty in a park, without the risk of serious fighting which often proves fatal.

It should be added that Peafowl are strong fliers and exceedingly active and it is very difficult to confine them in a garden or park if they decide to stray. Even with one wing clipped, they will easily leap to the top of a 6 ft fence or into the branches of a tree. They prefer to roost high above the ground and a hen will lead her chicks to a high branch at night as soon as they begin to fly which they will do at an early stage in their development.

# PIGEONS AND DOVES

**Waalia Fruit Pigeon** (Yellow-bellied Pigeon) *Treron waalia*
*Origin* Savannah regions of northern Africa and south-western Arabia

12 in. *Cock:* Neck, upper tail coverts and flanks grey-green, remainder of upper parts dark yellow-green. Breast and belly yellow. Under-tail coverts grey-green and brown-red with white margins. Wings brown, wine-red and dark yellow-green. Eye blue with yellow and wine-red rim, bill blue-grey with a reddish wax-like base. Legs yellow. *Hen:* Smaller and less red on wings.

Few fanciers will be able to keep these pigeons in their aviary, as the feeding is complicated and requires very special care. Boiled rice, boiled potatoes, white bread, hard-boiled egg, dates, figs, various seeds like paddy rice, canary seed and white millet will be needed, as well as fresh fruit. The birds eat rather a lot and need warmth. They can be kept in a large cage, but are apt quickly to become sluggish and over-fat. They have an unusual habit of depositing their excreta always in one spot and this facilitates cleaning.

They can be kept outside only during the summer months; as soon as the days become inclement or damp they must be brought indoors.

Breeding results are unknown.

**Charming Fruit Pigeon** (Purple-bellied Fruit Pigeon) *Ptilinopus bellus*
*Origin* New Guinea.

9¾ in. *Cock:* Bronze-green; forehead purple-red, nape and sides of head brighter green with purple on lower breast, a wide yellow band across breast which tends towards white at ends. Belly and under tail coverts green and flights have yellow margins. Eye and bill yellow, legs red. *Hen:* Green without the purple and yellow.

Fruit Pigeons are not popular cage or aviary birds owing to the numerous difficulties which their keeping presents. This is a great pity, for with a practical arrangement of their enclosure these birds can give a great deal of pleasure.

Various fruits, as sweet as possible, with boiled rice, bread and milk, and honey, make up a menu which is readily accepted.

These birds may be kept quite well in company with others in the outside aviary during the summer, but they do not tolerate others of their own kind.

There is no record of this species having bred in captivity but a rather similar species, the Lilac-crowned Fruit Pigeon, *Ptilinopus coronulatus*, is said to have been bred on the Continent. The birds nested year after year in a heated indoor aviary, building in an open nest box. The clutch consists of one egg only and the young mature quickly, leaving the nest at two weeks old.

They can be kept outside during the summer, but as soon as the cold weather arrives they must be taken indoors. They will live for many years.

**Triangular-spotted Pigeon** (Speckled Pigeon, Guinea Pigeon) *Columba guinea* Pl. 27
*Origin* Africa, n. of the rainforest and s. of the Sahara. Rhodesia, S. Africa.

Nearly 13 in. *Cock:* Head grey, neck feathers red-brown with grey tips and a green lustre. Back rich red-brown. Rump and secondaries also under parts grey. Wings as the back, with numerous triangular white spots, the remainder grey, tail grey with a white band across the tip. Bill black, legs red, eye red-brown and broad naked orbital ring red. *Hen:* Smaller.

This is one of the larger species of true pigeons but requires a spacious aviary but may safely be associated with other birds and even with its own kind.

It breeds readily. The diet should consist of various kinds of seed, including oats, broken maize and millet and canary seed, and also green food and insects, worms and snails. The birds may remain out-of-doors during the winter and may fly at liberty in summer, once they have started to nest.

## White-crowned Pigeon *Columba leucocephala* Pl 26
*Origin* West Indies, Cuba.

Nearly 14 in. *Cock* and *Hen* alike: Crown white, with a red-brown spot on nape. Neck feathers scale-like with a metallic gloss. Remainder dark grey lighter towards the belly. Eye light brown, eye cere red. Bill greenish-white with a reddish waxy overlay. Legs red.

These pigeons are suitable to keep with other large birds, also the larger parrakeets, and since they are gregarious by nature may also be kept with other pairs of their own kind, if a very roomy aviary is available. They will soon begin to breed and will make a loose nest which must be strengthened by a piece of wire netting placed under it. Care and treatment as for other pigeons.

## Carolina Dove *Zenaidura macroura carolinensis*
*Origin* Eastern States of North America.

12 in. *Cock:* Forehead and sides of head light brown. Neck and crown grey, with a black spot below the ear coverts, throat yellow-brown, breast vinaceous with a metallic violet spot on each side of neck. Under parts yellowish-white, upper parts greyish-brown, wings brown with black spots and grey with white tips. Eyes brown, eye cere is grey-blue. Bill black, red at root, legs lacquer-red. *Hen:* Smaller and duller in colouring, especially under parts.

These doves are very common in parks and gardens in their native country and are easily induced to breed in captivity. All manner of seeds, as well as peas, lots of insects and a quantity of green food form their diet. They will build only a little above the ground in a dense bush or shrub, sometimes even in a hole in the ground. Cock and hen take it in turns to incubate and both feed the young. As many as 3 families may be raised in one season, and nesting commences in March.

They are able to winter in the outside aviary.

This is a sub-species of *Z.m.macroura*, the Mourning Dove, which comes from the Greater Antilles and is very similar in appearance.

## Namaqua Dove (Cape Dove) *Oena capensis*

*Origin* Senegal and Egyptian Sudan. South to the Cape, Arabia and Aden.

*Cock:* Whole front is black, sharply defined against soft grey. Back is brown-grey. Rump striped black and white, under tail coverts black.

*Hen:* Is soft brown-grey, lighter on the abdomen.

These doves can be recommended for housing with small foreign finches as they are peaceable and soon become tame.

They are easily catered for and eat mainly seed, a mealworm or two, some ants' eggs and green stuff.

A small tray of wire netting or of woven twigs should be provided, on which they can place their flimsy and untidy nest. Without this support the nest is apt to fall to pieces and the eggs or young be destroyed.

When displaying, the cock will perform a kind of dance as he gracefully trips round his hen. These birds can nearly always be found on the ground amongst the grass and shrubs where they search for seeds and insects.

During the breeding season mostly late summer, the cock calls with a melodious 'coorrooroo', while he fans his tail and holds it high. Incubation takes a fortnight and there are usually several broods in a year.

**Laughing Dove** *Turtur senegalensis* (*Streptopelia senegalensis*)
*Origin* Widely distributed in Africa.

10 in. *Cock:* Throat, head and chest reddish brown. Collar black, each feather tipped with red-brown. Upper side red-brown merging into grey. Chin white, abdomen white. Eyes brown with red eyelids. Bill black, legs red. *Hen* is mostly grey in colour.

This bird is seldom imported, which is a great pity as it is so suitable to mix with other species in a flight. It cannot, however, be kept with its own kind.

In a pine tree Laughing Doves will soon build a slovenly nest, made of twigs and straw; this should be rein-

forced with wire netting, as it is apt to fall to pieces. Cock and hen take turns at incubation and as a rule the cock will feed the hen. The eggs hatch after 13 days and the young will fly after a further 12 days. They soon become independent and must then be separated, as their parents will have already started a new brood. They will become very tame and are much livelier than many of the other doves. With any luck, they will rear 5 to 6 broods in one season, each brood consisting of 2 chicks which usually prove to be cock and hen.

**Chinese Necklaced Dove** *Streptopelia chinensis* Pl. 25
*Origin* China, including Formosa and Hainan.

13½ in. *Cock:* Head grey, lighter on the forehead, nape pale vinaceous. A wide black 'necklace' with white spots. Light brown upper parts, grey under tail coverts, remainder of the under parts vinaceous, lighter on chin and belly. Wings dark grey with lighter margins and brown. Some feathers have white tips. Eye orange-brown with orange orbital ring. Bill black, legs red. *Hen:* Smaller and on the whole lighter in colouring.

There are several races of this dove, widely distributed in Asia; they all bear a close resemblance to one another and their treatment is exactly the same. There are closely related species in West Africa, and also from India. The latter may be recognized by the under tail coverts being white instead of grey.

They must be fed on various millets, oats and hemp. Green food and insects are less important. They are pretty and charming in the aviary and never disturb other birds. They spend much time searching on the ground for seeds and grit. They will build in a nest box or on a wire mesh platform in a shrub. The nest will consist of twigs put together in an untidy fashion. They will sit only if they are not disturbed; at the least noise they will leave the nest and if frequently disturbed will desert their eggs.

## Zebra Dove *Geopelia striata striata*
*Origin* India and Indonesia.

9 in. *Cock:* Forehead and throat grey. Nape pink, neck, breast and side of the head fine black-and-white horizontal stripes. Breast fawn, abdomen white. Wings brown with black stripes. Tail dusky with white spots. Bill and eyes brown-grey. Legs red. *Hen:* Similar but somewhat smaller than the cock, and duller in colouring.

Treatment as recommended for other small doves.

It is difficult to select a true pair, as the cock can only be distinguished by his display and behaviour towards a hen. Some people consider these birds dull and uninteresting as they seem to sit still all day on a nest box, and fly only when they are frightened. But in fact they can be most fascinating occupants of the aviary especially when they start breeding.

It is important to avoid any sudden movement when near them, as they are inclined to take fright and will fly round the aviary in a panic and may injure themselves against the wire.

When winter comes they must be brought indoors into a moderately-heated room. They are less hardy than the Diamond Dove.

## Diamond Dove *Geopelia c. cuneata*
*Origin* Australia. Pl. 28

The smallest of the doves, only slightly over 7½ in., the tail being more than half the total length. *Cock:* Head, neck and breast pale silvery grey; nape and back pale brown; wing coverts dark grey, each feather having a round white spot near the end; tail, central feathers dark grey and blackish towards the tips, outer feathers tipped with white; abdomen and under tail coverts white. Eyes orange-yellow to red surrounded by a bright coral-red ring; beak dark olive-brown; legs and feet reddish-flesh coloured. *Hen:* Slightly smaller with a distinctly finer head; eye ring not so pronounced and the upper parts more brown in tone. Sometimes, but not always, the white spots on the wings are less conspicuous.

These birds, one of the smallest species of dove, are very suitable for keeping together with small finches in a large flight where they will always be busy rummaging about on the ground. They will soon begin to breed well if a true pair has been obtained. The cock is recognizable only by his action of spreading his tail when displaying to a hen and by the blue-grey colouring of his back and wings which are brownish in the hen. Another difference, only noticeable during the breeding period, is that the deep red orbital ring of the cock is wider than that of the hen.

Usually from the normal clutch of 2 eggs, the 2 chicks will prove to be cock and hen. Brothers and sisters will pair together, and, so long as the quality does not deteriorate, a certain amount of inbreeding may be permitted. Now and again fresh blood must be introduced by purchase or exchange.

An artificial nest made of wire netting, covered with canvas and fixed on to horizontal branches of a pine tree, is appreciated; on this the doves will build with twigs, coarse grass and moss.

When displaying the cock dances round the hen with tail feathers fanned out, and will then beat his wings on the ground before mating. The birds take turns at incubation for 13 days.

As soon as the young become independent, they must be placed in another aviary, for the parents will begin a new nest at once and will then chase the young away.

It takes a little care to get a pair together, as the birds do not always agree at first, and many breeding efforts have failed for this reason. It may even be necessary to replace one of the pair with another bird of the same sex. There has also been excessive inbreeding which has weakened the stamina and fertility of some strains and it is as well to start with birds which are completely unrelated if possible. Several pairs cannot be kept together and an odd bird, if left with a pair, will be ruthlessly persecuted.

The best breeding time is in May, June, July and August, and the birds should be prevented from nesting in the other months. If necessary, the pairs should then be separated.

Food should consist mainly of seed, millet in various forms, canary seed, rape and maw-seed, together with weed seeds, as well as some insectivorous mixture, a mealworm or so and ants' eggs. Other insects are often appreciated. Green stuff is another necessity, and young cabbage leaves, chopped up finely, are always welcome. During the breeding time the birds need germinated seeds. Soaked stale bread is also used for rearing the young doves. There is usually surplus seed on the floor of an aviary, and it will probably have begun to germinate. The doves will take these seeds and plants in preference to the dry seed. Grit should never be forgotten.

It is safe to let these birds winter outside if shut in a well-protected shelter at night. They will also nest in a large cage in the house. This species deserves to be kept more extensively than it is at present.

**Peaceful Dove** *Geopelia striata placida*

*Origin* Australia.

8 in. *Cock:* Forehead, cheeks and throat grey, nape grey-brown, neck narrowly barred with black and white, back with dark barring. Breast vinaceous, shading into beige on the under parts. Bill blue-grey with a black tip. Legs grey. *Hen:* Somewhat smaller than cock.

These doves can well be kept in an aviary, together with small finches. They are easily tamed and are nearly always to be found on the ground. In addition to millets, they will eat grass and weed seeds.

Although breeding results have been obtained, they are not considered to be easy birds to breed. If it is desired to make an attempt, it is best to give the birds an open box filled with hay and hung up, not too high. A very quiet spot must be chosen, for the least noise will cause them to desert the nest. Although they need a good temperature to feel entirely happy, they have been wintered in a frost-proof room without any detrimental effects. A warm room is, however, very much better.

**Bar-shouldered Dove** *Geopelia humeralis*

*Origin* Australia.

11½ in. *Cock:* Head, throat and sides of the neck grey. Neck golden-brown, back duller brown, all feathers having black margins. Under parts pale vinaceous, belly white. Wings brown, tail grey-brown and chestnut-brown. Eyes brown-yellow with a purple orbital ring. Bill blue-grey, legs red. *Hen:* More grey on breast.

Unlike some others, these Doves are active, and will run about busily on the ground hunting for something edible. They stand our climate extremely well and can stay out-of-doors during the winter. They are mainly seed-eaters, and barely touch green food or fruit. Some insects will be eaten. They need space and are not suitable for a cage, but can quite well be kept together with other birds, except in the breeding season, when the cock becomes fierce towards his own kind. They breed late in the year and take turns at incubation. They grow very tame and require the same treatment as does the Diamond Dove. The nest needs to be supported with a piece of wire mesh. The young leave the nest only 12 days after hatching.

**Pigmy Dove** *Columbigallina minuta*
*Origin* Brazil, Peru

6 in. *Cock:* Crown neck and upper tail coverts grey. Nape brownish, forehead with a vinaceous sheen, back grey-brown. Neck and breast vinaceous, blending into grey-white on belly. Wings brown, black and grey, tail grey and brown with white towards the tip. Bill brown, eye red, legs flesh-coloured. *Hen:* Upper parts lighter, throat and belly whitish, breast and sides grey-brown.

These doves are really only happy when kept warm. They can be safely associated with small foreign finches. They are quiet and spend much time on the ground. They should be fed on mixed seeds and small insects. They will make a nest in an open nest box. Cock and hen will take turns at incubation which lasts for 16 days.

Pigmy Doves are extremely suitable for the living-room as their soft cooing is never irritating. They soon grow tame but must be carefully accustomed to their new surroundings; at first they will be shy and inclined to fly upwards when approached.

**Blue-spotted Dove** (Sapphire-spotted Dove) *Turtur afer*
*Origin* Gambia to Portuguese Guinea.

8 in. *Cock:* Forehead white, crown grey, cheeks vinaceous, remainder of head being grey. Neck and back brown-grey, with two black cross bars on the rump and a brown band across the middle. Breast vinaceous, belly white, wings brown-grey, with metallic blue spots. Flights brown with dark margins. Eyes brown, bill black with a lighter tip, legs flesh-coloured. *Hen:* Is paler in colour and somewhat smaller in size.

Various sub-species, such as the Red-billed Dove, *T. afer kilimensis,* are sometimes offered.

Few fanciers seem to appreciate these little doves yet they are comparatively inexpensive and are neither restive nor do they disturb any of the other occupants of an aviary. They will nest in a low pine tree and will raise three families in a season.

They are very well able to withstand the vagaries of our climate. As well as seed they like to eat many weed seeds, much green food chopped up, a meal-worm now and again, and they are very fond of ants' eggs, also brown breadcrumbs and groats, wheat and maize. All kind of insects, and also snails, are a treat for them.

Incubation lasts a fortnight. The nest must be supported with a piece of wire netting. Their voice is soft and during the summer may frequently be heard at night.

**Indian Green-winged Dove** (Emerald Dove) *Chalcophaps indica* Pl. 30
*Origin* India.

Nearly 11 in. *Cock:* Forehead and eyebrow stripe white, head and neck grey, sides of head, hind neck and breast deep vinaceous. Under parts grey. Mantle grey with a golden-green sheen, lower part of the back black-grey with light-grey cross bars and a bronze sheen. Wings irridescent golden-green, flights red-brown. Tail black. Eyes brown, bill red, legs red. *Hen:* Forehead dull grey and the eyebrow stripe narrower; crown, nape and upper back brown; under surface reddish-brown lightly speckled with grey; shoulder brown; tail, four central feathers brownish-black, followed by 2 on each side with a chestnut tinge towards the base and the outer feathers grey with a black band towards the tip.

These Doves are usually available on the market, and two closely related species, the Australian Green-winged Dove, *Chalcophaps stephani*, and the Philippine Green-winged Dove, *Chalcophaps natalis philipinus*, both of which are very similar to the Indian in appearance, have been imported.

This species does not need a great deal of attention, especially if kept in a large aviary. They do not interfere with other birds, run actively and busily on the ground in search of seeds

and insects, and enjoy eating berries, fruit and also green food.

At other times they will sit perched quietly on a branch for hours at a time, and this habit has gained for them, as Zebra Doves, a reputation of being dull and uninteresting.

They will breed well in an aviary but must be able to build high up, sometimes using the top of a nest box. The nest will be made carelessly and slovenly, as are all doves' nests; but it is usually a trifle more bowl-shaped than that of the other species so that the danger of the eggs falling out is a little less.

**Bronze-winged Pigeon** *Phaps chalcoptera* Pl. 31
*Origin* Australia generally, and Tasmania.

14 in. *Cock:* Buff-white forehead, crown and nape brown with a purple gloss on the side of the head, lores black. Cheeks, ear coverts and neck grey, with a pale buff stripe running above and below eye. Throat white, upper parts brown-grey, the feathers margined with buff, under parts wine-red merging into grey. Wings brown-grey with metallic bronze and green spots. Eye red-brown, bill grey-black, legs red. *Hen:* Paler in colour, grey forehead, spots on wings golden-green.

This species requires a large and roomy aviary and if the accommodation is to be shared the other inhabitants must be large enough to defend themselves against the cock which is apt to be fierce during the mating season. A very similar and closely related species from the Philippines is sometimes available.

These birds eat mainly seed farinaceous seeds for preference, and they are liable to become over-fat. Special care must be taken to prevent this as it is apt to have an adverse influence on the breeding. They build a slovenly nest in a low bush or on a shelf or will use an open nest box. They will rear at least two families per season.

**Brush Bronze-winged Pigeon** *Phaps elegans*
*Origin* Southern Australia and Tasmania.

13½ in. *Cock:* Head, neck and entire under parts grey. Forehead yellow-brown, a wide chestnut-brown band runs from eye to eye across the nape. Cheek and ear coverts white, neck and upper back brown. Scapulars and the remainder of the upper parts olive-grey with a red-brown spot on throat. Brownish sheen on belly. Wings grey with 2 broad copper-green and purple metallic bands. Eye brown, legs purple-red. *Hen:* Much duller in colour than the cock.

These pigeons are mainly seed-eaters, although berries and small insects are appreciated.

Breeding results have repeatedly been obtained. During the breeding season the cock is rather pugnacious. These birds give little trouble in an aviary; their nest will be built low down in a bush or shrub.

**Crested Bronze-winged Pigeon**
(Australian Crested Pigeon) *Ocyphaps lophotes* Pl. 33
*Origin* South Queensland, New South Wales, Victoria and South Australia.

About 13 in. Lighter in build than the preceding species and with much longer tail. *Cock:* Head, breast and abdomen grey; high, pointed crest black, upper parts olivaceous grey; upper tail coverts tipped with white; sides of neck and breast with pink flush; wing coverts sandy-grey to pure grey, each feather with a subterminal black band; greater coverts metallic green with white borders, primaries dull brownish-black, secondaries with metallic purple and blue broadly edged with white; tail blackish-brown faintly washed with purple, blue and green on the outer webs; beak blackish; legs and feet crimson; eyes orange surrounded by reddish naked skin. *Hen:* Very difficult to distinguish—usually slightly smaller with finer head and narrower neck. The display of the cock during courting may help to distinguish the sexes.

Never plentiful, these birds are, however, usually more readily obtainable than the two Australian species previously mentioned. The birds are certainly interesting and hardy.

Pairs of these pigeons may safely be kept with other birds; it is only with their own and closely related species that constant quarrelling may be expected. They will nest quite readily especially if suitable platforms are fixed in the aviary on which they can build. They like to make their slovenly nest in an open nest box or shallow tray such as a cigar box fixed to the wall and partly screened with heather or fir branches, but boxes of open pattern should have one or two holes in the bottom to allow rain water to escape.

They share incubation, but the cock sits only during the afternoon; the hen sitting the rest of the day and all night. The incubation period is 18 to 20 days. The young fly 20 days after hatching.

Diet required is the same as for the Diamond Dove.

**White-bellied Dove** (Jamaican Ground Dove) *Leptotila jamaicensis*
Pl. 29
*Origin* West Indies.

12–13 in. *Cock:* Forehead white; crown ash-grey; back and sides of neck metallic pink with gold and green iridescence; back and wings olive-brown; cheeks, throat and whole of under parts white; tail, two central feathers olive, remainder grey-brown with white tips. *Hen:* Smaller than cock, forehead greyish and the white parts less pure, having a greyish or buff tone.

This species is of a particularly gentle and peaceful nature and as it spends most of its time on the ground, it is a suitable subject to be included in a mixed collection. It is reasonably hardy when once acclimatized but dislikes damp and should be provided with a frost-proof shelter during the winter months. Mixed seeds including millet, dari, small wheat and groats form a suitable staple diet and, for a change, fruit pips such as orange and apple, and cut-up peanuts are appreciated. A certain amount of green stuff is also eaten and probably small insects.

The nest, a flimsy platform of twigs and leaves, is usually placed in a shrub near to the ground and incubation of the 2 white eggs takes 16 days. In addition to the seed mixture and green stuff, canary rearing food or soaked biscuit crumbs should be offered when young are being reared. This species breeds fairly readily in captivity and it was first bred in 1903 in England.

It is advisable to restrict their breeding to the spring and summer months. Four nests a year are no exception and usually 2 youngsters are hatched per nest.

When independent the young should be placed in a separate cage or aviary. Like the Diamond Dove, this species is worthy of much more interest than is at present shown in it.

**Blue-headed Quail Dove** *Starnoenas cyanocephala*
*Origin* Cuba.

12 in. *Cock* and *Hen* alike: Crown grey bordered by a black band. White stripe from chin under eye to nape and a black stripe passing through eye. Upper parts olive-grey, throat, head and upper breast black, bordered with white. Under parts brown, breast rosy. Wings brown with lighter margins. Bill red with a blue-grey tip. Legs red with blue edges to the scales.

Their slow movements and long periods of inactivity perched with fluffed-out feathers tends to make these birds rather dull occupants of the aviary. Only on warm sunny summer days do they really seem to come to life.

As might be expected, they cause little trouble in a mixed collection. They eat seeds and insects, berries and green food. Breeding is not difficult.

**Bleeding-heart Pigeon**
*Gallicolumba luzonica* Pl. 32
*Origin* Philippines.

10 in. *Cock:* Forehead and crown pale grey, merging into dark grey towards back and tail. A green and reddish sheen over feathers. Cheeks, breast and throat white, with a blood-red spot in centre of breast. Belly yellow-white to white. Wings grey with brown and a black cross band just in front of the tips. Eye brown-black, legs purple-red. *Hen:* Smaller red spot on breast and generally more buff on under parts.

These pigeons, which are usually

active, running about on the ground, can be kept together with larger birds. They will probably not molest birds of other species, but there is usually disagreement with others of their own kind. Some pairs are peaceful, others pugnacious; it all depends on the temperament of the cock.

Care is needed in acclimatization, especially at first. They eat, in addition to millet, canary seed, oats, wheat and hemp, stale white bread with grated carrot. They may not always accept mealworms but as true ground birds they will hunt diligently for all manner of insects, snails, spiders and worms.

They are not very quick to start breeding. It is important to have a well-planted aviary with a number of dense shrubs where it is possible to fix a wire mesh support for a nest. It is advisable to supply some straw and twigs as nesting material. The pigeons prefer a nesting place not too high above the ground. The cock will bring the material and the hen will try to produce a little order out of the chaos of twigs and other materials, but the ultimate result will be a really slovenly nest. If the nest is fixed too high up the cock will fly up high too, and chase other high nesting birds.

The cock changes places regularly with his hen during incubation. Usually he sits on the 2 eggs during the day. The hen, while on the nest, is regularly fed by him. Hatching is not always successful; often the chicks do not develop fully or fail to emerge. Attempts have been made to get the eggs hatched by ordinary domestic pigeons, and these have succeeded in many instances. Quite a number of Bleeding-heart Pigeons can be reared in this way in a season. If the luck has been favourable and fertile eggs obtained, the cock and hen should be separated during the winter months, otherwise the hen will exhaust herself by continuous laying.

During the rearing time, the parents will eat quantities of insect food and an extra ration of mealworms is needed; ants' eggs and egg food are also consumed avidly. Incubation lasts a fortnight; the squabs, usually 2 in number, will leave the nest after another 10 days. They are at first very timid. The colouring of the nest feathers is dull brown but after 6 weeks the distinctive red spot on the breast becomes visible and in another 10 weeks there is no noticeable difference between old and young.

The birds are hardy and can winter out-of-doors, but they must be able to roost in a shelter. Very early in spring, February–March, preparation must be made for breeding. Lime and grit should always be available and cod liver oil should be added to the seed mixture.

# WATERFOWL

**White-faced Tree Duck** (White-faced Whistling Duck) *Dendrocygna viduata* Pl. 34
*Origin* Tropical South America and Africa, south of the Sahara, Madagascar and Comoro Islands.

*Drake* and *Duck* alike but the duck may be slightly smaller. Crown, forehead, face, chin and throat pure white; nape and back of neck black; remainder of plumage warm brown, the feathers of the back being lanceolated and streaked with buff; sides of breast and flanks finely barred with buff and black; belly very dark brown to blackish; beak black; legs and feet dark grey; eyes dark brown.

The distribution of this species is without parallel among birds, with the exception of the Fulvous Tree Duck, being found throughout both tropical Africa and South America. It is usually extremely tame and a delightful addition to any collection of waterfowl, seldom straying even when allowed at liberty, full winged. It is, however, inclined to be sensitive to severe cold and is better kept in an enclosed pen during the winter. Feeding and treatment as described for the Red-billed Tree Duck.

**Red-billed Tree Duck** (Red-billed Whistling Duck) *Dendrocygna autumnalis autumnalis* Pl. 36, 37
*Origin* Mexico and Central America

*Drake* and *Duck* alike but the duck a little smaller. Forehead greyish, crown and a line running down back of neck dark brown to black; remainder of head, throat and upper neck grey;

lower neck and chest dark, warm brown; remainder of under parts black. Back and wings dark brown, the latter with a prominent white patch; tail black; eyes dark brown; beak red. Long legs and feet pink.

The deportment of these ducks, which are fairly long-legged, is distinctive and upright. They have a quaint whistling call note like a high pitched 'breereereeree'.

'Whistling goose' would be a good descriptive name for them. They will sit or roost in trees occasionally, but seldom, if ever, nest off the ground. The duck will begin to lay in May in a specially constructed nest box similar to a small dog kennel, but she will not readily sit. The eggs may be incubated by a bantam hen and the ducklings will hatch in 27 days. Their rearing is as described for Mandarin Ducks (p. 157). It is essential to guard the youngsters from damp, which causes many deaths. During rainy weather they should be kept in a hen-house or dry shed.

It is only when they are completely feathered that they can withstand the vicissitudes of the weather. They will eat all manner of green food, berries and grain, and need a similar menu as that described for other ducks. During frosty weather they should be placed in a shed or barn. They soon become very friendly and will associate with other ducks.

**Northern Common) Pintail** *Anas acuta acuta* Pl. 38, 39
*Origin* Europe, Asia and N. America.

*Drake:* Whole of head and throat

warm brown; a broad line of blackish-brown running down the back of the neck from the nape to the shoulder; white line on the sides of the neck joining the pure white breast and abdomen; back and flanks vermiculated grey; ventral feathers yellowish buff; upper and under tail coverts black; mantle feathers elongated, white with broad blue-black shaft stripes; reddish speculum on wings; tail black, central feathers greatly elongated. Beak dark grey, legs and feet blackish; eyes hazel. The drake in eclipse plumage is much like the duck but there is a boldness about his appearance which will usually distinguish him from his mate. *Duck:* General colour fawn mottled and streaked with varying shades of brown; the line down the back of the neck less defined and the central tail feathers not so long as those of the drake. This species is hardy and does well in confinement on the diet described for other ducks.

## Common Sheld-Duck *Tadorna tadorna* Pl. 40

*Origin* Western Europe, Siberia, Mongolia and Tibet.

*Drake:* Head and neck black with rich dark green sheen as also are a band across shoulders, tips of wings and tail; green and reddish speculum and a broad chestnut band round back and chest; under tail coverts dark brown; remainder of plumage pure white; eyes brown; beak bright red and having a swollen caruncle; legs and feet pink. During the eclipse period the drake loses the caruncle. *Duck:* Very like the drake but lacking the caruncle and slightly smaller. After the summer moult the feathers of the face turn light grey and it is therefore possible to distinguish the sexes at all seasons. In a wild state the Shelduck prefers the sea coast and salt water and feeds largely on small molluscs and crustaceans. It will however adapt itself to captivity readily but should be provided with a regular supply of live food especially when ducklings are to be reared. They nest in holes in the ground and in captivity it is as well to provide artificial burrows consisting of large wooden boxes buried in the ground, with tunnel entrances which can be made with concrete drain pipes of a suitable dimension. Glazed pipes should not be used as the slippery surface will discourage the duck from entering. If these birds are to be kept at liberty in a park or garden, or confined to an open-topped enclosure, they must be pinioned otherwise they will soon stray. They are quite hardy and are not, as a rule, dangerous in a mixed collection, although they may show a tendency to bully other and less robust species.

## Muscovy Duck *Cairina moschata* Pl. 35

*Origin* Central and South America.

*Drake:* The wild bird is dark brown with a beautiful green and purple sheen and with the wing coverts white. The bill is black and rose-coloured, and has a red boss on base in front of nostrils. Eyes yellow-brown and feet black. Unfortunately domestication and interbreeding has produced a coarse, ugly strain in which the wattles are much enlarged and the true colour replaced by white, black or black and white pied. *Duck:* Similar but much smaller and lacks the red boss on bill.

This is one of the most remarkable ducks; indeed it looks more like a goose than a duck. It may weigh up to nearly 10 lb. As a rule drakes of most species can be distinguished by their curled tail feathers, but not so with the Muscovy, the drake only being recognizable by his far superior size.

They are mainly grass-eaters. The duck will lay freely and sit well and the eggs take 36 days to hatch. The ducklings mature slowly and will not be full fledged in less than 16 weeks, unlike most other species of duck which feather in three months.

A cross between a Muscovy and a Pekin Duck produces infertile young and this again suggests that this species is not a true duck. It owes its name to the presence of a gland which gives off such a strong odour of musk that the flesh is uneatable unless the gland is removed and the bird beheaded immediately it is killed. The bird also has peculiar fleshy red warts on the head which are said to spread the musk-like odour.

The species is mute but the drakes may be recognized not only by their size but also by the presence of a red boss between the base of the bill and the nostrils. If it is intended to let the Muscovy run with other ducks, care should be taken to ensure that each drake has a duck of its own, as unpaired drakes will cause endless trouble in the flock. They like to roost in the open on horizontal tree trunks.

The ducks have a reputation for long and patient sitting and eggs which are on the point of hatching may be removed from the nest to an incubator and replaced by fresh eggs on which the duck will continue to sit until incubation is complete.

Muscovys need the same care and feeding as other ducks and one drake may be kept with as many as 8 ducks.

**Mandarin Duck** *Aix galericulata* Pl. 42
*Origin* China, Formosa, Japan.

*Drake:* In breeding plumage, crown and long sweeping crest extending onto nape, greenish-black at front fading to bright chestnut and terminating greenish-black; sides of head pure white extending back to tip of crest, stained warm chestnut before the eyes; cheeks and side of neck, elongated feathers forming a mane of rich chestnut striated with fine, white lines; hind neck and mantle rich metallic dark green; back, tail coverts and tail dark brown; chest rich purplish-brown, divided from whitish breast by a broad band of white with triple greenish-black bars each side; sides and flanks darker brown, finely pencilled with black and terminated by a broad white and black band, the latter with metallic green reflections. Standing above the sides are two greatly developed fans of bright chestnut feathers having the appearance of sails. This form of ornamentation is unique to the Mandarin drakes. Beak orange-red; legs and feet yellow; eyes dark brown. In eclipse the drake resembles the duck but has a paler face and retains the red beak. *Duck:* Head and depressed crest dark brown but with pronounced white eyebrow stripe which makes identification fairly easy; throat whitish, neck, breast and under parts dull brown mottled with greyish-white. Wing coverts warm brown, flights blackish-brown with whitish margins; beak blackish with almost white tip; legs and feet blackish. This species is probably the most beautiful of all waterfowl.

This is a species of duck which nests in hollow trees well above the ground level. Its nest box, which should be at least 10 in. square and lined with damp peat dust and dead leaves, should therefore be placed on a pole, about 2 to 3 ft above the ground, with a tree trunk or small ladder by which the bird can reach the entrance.

The duck will lay 6–12 eggs in the nest box and will surround them with a layer of down plucked from her own body. Incubation lasts a month or even longer. When the ducklings hatch, she will oil their down thoroughly with oil from her own oil gland and when she coaxes them from the nest they just tumble to the ground. Strange to say, they seldom suffer any injury. If the eggs have been hatched under a hen or in an incubator, due account must be taken of the fact that the little ones have not been oiled, and therefore must not enter the water during the first few days, until their own oil glands begin to operate, otherwise they will become water-logged and may be drowned.

With the aid of ants' eggs and special duck-rearing food, the young ducklings will grow rapidly. Green food, chopped-up nettles, lettuce and chickweed, together with mashed hard-boiled egg, may also be given, and later shrimp meal and maize meal. Mandarin ducks are very fond of earthworms and it is advisable to give some to the ducklings when they are a few weeks old. During the summer other worms or maggots may be found, especially in mushrooms. The mushrooms should be placed in a dry box for a day and then the hoods and stems should be cut through. A writhing mass of maggots will be exposed. The ducklings are very fond of these.

**Carolina Duck** (Wood Duck) *Aix sponsa* Pl. 43
*Origin* North America.

*Drake:* In breeding plumage, crown feathers extending into long crest lying flat over the nape, metallic dark green with purple reflections; narrow white lines extending from nostrils to nape and from behind the eyes; ear coverts and cheeks violet divided by a white line curving down from below the eye and joining the white chin and throat and white collar, wings rich shining green and purple, breast rich purple-brown spangled with small white spots and outlined with white; back and upper tail coverts metallic green and violet; tail blackish; under tail coverts chestnut, belly greyish-brown fading to white; sides warm brown divided from ventral feathers by broad white and black bands and with black and white crescents on upper border; beak dark brown, orange-scarlet at base of upper mandible; legs and feet yellow; eyes dark brown surrounded by ring of scarlet naked skin. In eclipse the drake is much like the duck but retains rather more colour on the crown and back. *Duck:* Mainly brown, dark on crown and nape, dull greyish-brown on cheeks, warm on back and wings with slight green and purple sheen; chin and throat greyish-white; under parts dull brown with pale whitish spots on sides; beak dull black; legs and feet dull brownish-black. These birds will become quite tame, and can run about quite freely in the garden, even associating with domestic poultry. They are very hardy and even during the winter will run about happily in the snow and will roost under any low conifers or thick bushes. A small pond is a necessity as the actual mating takes place on the water. The behaviour and display of the drake are interesting and amusing to watch. During May, and sometimes even in April, the duck will begin to lay and as it is the habit of ducks to nest in holes in trees at some considerable height, a small barrel or nest box should be provided on a platform raised well above the ground, with a sloping board up which the duck can scramble. The box should be lined with hay and damp wood chips or peat.

They like to eat berries, insects, snails and worms and also acorns and beech mast. Green food and grain should also figure on their menu. Incubation takes a month. The rearing of the ducklings is similar to that of the Mandarin Ducks.

**Red-crested Pochard** *Netta rufina* Pl. 41

*Origin* Eastern Europe and Asia.

*Drake:* Head and throat a mass of soft bright chestnut feathers; back of neck, chest and breast, and also vent, upper and under tail coverts and the short tail velvety-black with greenish sheen; mantle dull brown; shoulders and flanks white; eyes, beak and legs red. In eclipse plumage drake is similar to duck. *Duck:* Entirely dull brown, the cheeks, upper breast and flanks pale greyish-brown; bill, legs and feet blackish.

Although one of the Diving Ducks, the Red-crested Pochard does not dive much and is said to readily adapt itself to confinement and to the normal treatment for other ducks. It is hardy and breeds readily.

---

# PARROTS AND PARROT-LIKE SPECIES

**Ornate Lorikeet** (Ornamented Lorikeet) *Trichoglossus ornatus* Pl. 54.
*Origin* Celebes, Buton and the Togian Islands.

Nearly 9 in. *Cock:* Crown and ear coverts purplish-blue; a band of red with transverse blue-black lines on occiput and a yellow line running down the sides of the neck; nape, back, tail, wings and abdomen bright green, the latter lightly barred with blue-black; flights blackish-green. Throat, cheeks and breast bright red, the breast lightly barred with bluish-black; flanks barred with light green and yellow. Beak orange, eyes hazel, feet grey. *Hen:* Similar and very difficult to distinguish – may be slightly smaller and with a more ladylike expression.

This species is sensitive to cold and although it may be kept in an aviary during the summer months it needs protection in the winter and is then better housed in a roomy cage indoors where the temperature can be maintained at a minimum of 55° F. (13° C.). Like most of the Lorikeets it is playful and usually very tame and will make a delightful pet if given constant attention.

The feeding should be as for the Varied Lorikeet (p. 160) and in addition it is advisable to supply nectar at all times.

It was first bred in France in 1883.

**Swainson's Lorikeet** (Blue Mountain Lorikeet, Rainbow Lorikeet) *Trichoglossus haematod moluccanus* Pl. 52
*Origin* Australia, Timor.

Nearly 12 in. *Cock:* Head and throat

purplish-blue: back, wings and tail green with a yellowish band on the nape; breast and under wing coverts vermilion red; belly bright blue; under tail coverts yellow tipped with green. A yellow band on the under surface of the wings. Beak orange-red tipped with yellow; feet dark grey. Irides reddish-brown. *Hen:* Similar but with finer beak and perhaps a little smaller.

In their natural habitat great flocks of these lorikeets visit the eucalyptus trees. They eat the blossoms and in their arrow-like flight they flash through the air like sparkling jewels. They make an ear-piercing noise when eating, and while in flight they emit a shrill call. They eat nectar, flowers, fruit, grass seed and insects. As well as their piercing calls they have another great disadvantage. Their excreta is very fluid and voluminous; this is due to the diet they require in captivity which consists of much sweet fruit, seeds, soaked stale white bread covered with a lot of sugar or some honey, greens and vegetables. When attempts were made to accustom them to a different diet, such as hemp seed, the substance of the excreta became much firmer.

Their brush-like tongues indicate that they are essentially nectar feeders and it is better to clean out the roomy cage thoroughly every day and thus keep the birds in good condition, than to attempt to force them onto a dry and unnatural diet.

As they are very intolerant with other large parrots, pairs should be kept separately. If given a quiet spot and a large nesting box with an entrance of just over 3 in. diameter, there is a chance that they will breed. The hen incubates by herself, during which time the cock feeds her on the nest. The young are hatched out after a month and stay in the nest for another 2 months.

There may be 2 or even 3 broods in a season. The first breeding result was obtained in the United Kingdom in 1907.

For rearing the young the following diet should be available: rusks soaked in milk to which honey or a lot of sugar has been added, fresh chickweed, young corn on the cob and other ripening grain. As soon as the young come out of the nest, they should be given germinated seeds, which they will soon begin to eat by themselves.

The young birds can become exceedingly tame and learn to say their name and to speak a few words. Their playful behaviour is amusing to watch.

The species has been crossed with the Red-collared Lorikeet.

**Red-collared Lorikeet** *Trichoglossus haematod rubritorquis*
*Origin* North Western Australia.

Nearly 11 in. *Cock* and *Hen* alike: Head and throat blue, orange-red neck band, extending round nape, bordered by a broad blue band below. Breast orange-red like band around neck. All the upper parts green, belly blackish green. Flanks yellow flecked with red and green. Wings and tail green, beak red, eyes red, legs grey.

These birds, like other lorikeets, are only infrequently available and a pair, which is fairly expensive, is difficult to get.

They are nectar- and soft fruit-eaters and should have a roomy aviary, which must be kept thoroughly clean. Currants and raisins, together with other fruit, are a treat; bread and milk sweetened with sugar, some canary seed, hemp, with chickweed, make for a varied diet. These birds are also fond of millet in the spray. They become tame very readily and, except for their rather loud screeching, are attractive pets. They can winter in a frost-proof room.

Breeding has been repeatedly successful. During the rearing time they must be given germinated seeds and soaked baby rusks. Boiled rice with sugar and/ or honey, sometimes with an egg, and candied as well as fresh fruit should also figure on the menu. Fresh willow twigs or twigs from fruit trees should always be hung in the aviary. They love nibbling off every bit of bark. Some of this bark will be eaten and it seems essential for their well-being.

When first imported these lorikeets should be kept at a temperature of about 75°F (24°C) or well above normal room heating. Later on normal warmth is quite adequate. Only after they have become used to their food should the temperature be reduced. Once they have grown accustomed to an outside aviary, they may winter in an unheated room. They bathe extensively and really need to do so in order to keep their plumage free from the sticky juice of fruit and the honey on which they feed.

The first breeding was recorded in the United Kingdom in 1910. Crossings are recorded with Swainson's Lorikeet.

**Varied Lorikeet,** *Psitteuteles versicolor*
*Origin* Northwest Australia.

8½ in. *Cock* and *Hen* alike: A lovely grass-green, with wine-red on back and sides. The crown is scarlet, the nape, cheeks and neck are yellow and mauve, as is the upper breast. Band across the breast wine-red. The whole of the body plumage is more or less barred with green and yellow. Lacquer-red beak and grey legs.

In the natural state these lorikeets live mainly on nectar, which they extract from the flowers with their brush tongues. A good diet can be made up of baby rusks soaked in milk and mixed with honey, also stale white bread soaked in milk and covered with sugar, and soft and sweet fruit.

Like Swainson's Lorikeet, these birds also soil their cages badly and everything must be thoroughly cleaned daily. It might, therefore, be advisable to keep them in an outside flight with part roofed in to provide shelter. They are very hardy and will often be found roosting outside.

They sometimes start to nest in the middle of winter, but it is much better not to allow this until towards the end of March. In a nest box with an entrance hole of not more than 3 inches in diameter hung between shrubs, some damp moss and sawdust should be placed, as these birds have shown a a preference for this type of nest in which to deposit their eggs. The breeding and hatching are as described in the case of Swainson's Lorikeet. The first breeding result was recorded in the United Kingdom in 1936. A good rearing food can be prepared as follows: Mix some baby food with equal proportions of milk and water and boil for a very short time, adding sugar and honey. Add some pieces of stale white bread cut into smallish cubes. Boiled potatoes and sweet fresh fruit should also be supplied daily.

All surplus food should be removed towards evening or it will become sour.

**Purple-capped Lory** (Purple-naped Lory) *Domicella domicella*. Pl. 53
*Origin* Assam and Amboyna.

12 in. *Cock* and *Hen* alike: Crown of head black at front blending into deep

purple. Orange band across the upper breast, remainder deep velvety-red, darker on back with wings green and webs of the flights yellow. There is a small patch of pale blue on the bend of the wings and the thighs are rich cobalt. Tail red with a purple coloured band just above tip. Eyes brown, beak orange, legs black.

The care of lorikeets and lories is always more complicated than that of other parrakeets or parrots, for the food, consisting of boiled rice, sweetened bread-and-milk, sponge cake, seeds and fruit, causes liquid excreta so the cage needs regular cleaning.

They possess many good qualities which mark them out as cage birds. They learn rapidly, grow tame quickly, and soon cease their screeching. They like to be petted and will perch on the shoulder and beg for a tit-bit in the shape of a grape or a piece of soft fruit.

Lories roost in holes in trees and for this reason they should have a nest box or hollow log available throughout the year. Breeding results have been obtained. The normal clutch consists of 2 eggs only and these the hen will hatch in 25 days. The young only become covered with down after 3 weeks and will not leave the nest box until nearly 4 months old. They then quickly become independent. They are paler in colour than their parents for the first 4 months and have black beaks.

The species is double-brooded. First breeding recorded, Belgium, 1916.

If it is not desired to keep the birds indoors, they are still well worth having as they can stand a low temperature when once acclimatized and are therefore, equally suited to life in an aviary. During the winter the accommodation must at least be frost-proof; for preference the shelter should be heated.

**Chattering Lory** *Domicella garrula garrula*
*Origin* Halmahera – Indonesia.

11½ in. *Cock* and *Hen* alike. Deep velvety-crimson with green wings, the bend of the wings being yellow; basal half of tail red, distal half purple tinged with green; base of primaries red; under wing coverts yellow. There is a narrow yellow band across the shoulders. Eyes deep yellow; beak red; legs and feet dusky.

This lory requires the same treatment as the Purple-capped Lory. It can safely be kept in an outdoor aviary during the summer months and although it cannot be described as a free breeder, there is always a fair chance that it may nest. Young have been successfully reared in Europe and it is also said to have crossed with Swainson's Lorikeet. During the winter months it should be kept in a heated, indoor enclosure but it is not suitable to have in a living-room as its voice is harsh and it is apt to scream continuously. A subspecies, the Yellow-backed Lory, *D.g. flavopalliata*, is at present more frequently available than the Chattering Lory from which it differs only in having a large yellow patch on the mantle (Pl. 55). It comes from the Molluccas and requires exactly the same treatment.

**Musk Lorikeet** *Glossopsitta concinna*
*Origin* Australia.

Nearly 11 in. *Cock* and *Hen* alike. Forehead, lores and ear coverts, red. Crown green with a blue gloss; neck dull olive-brown-yellow. Breast yellow, remainder being green. Eyes brown-yellow, beak black, legs grey.

These birds may be kept in a large cage but a bird-room suits them much better. Breeding results have been obtained. A large nest box, 10 by 10 by 16 in., should be placed on the floor. Rearing food must be supplied in the shape of soaked rusks with honey and sugar, canary seed, soaked currants and raisins, millet in the spray and quantities of green food. Soaked seeds, baby rusks, and later on some hemp seed, should also figure on the menu. Their care and upkeep is as for other lorikeets. The first breeding results were reported in Germany in 1903 and in Britain in 1930. Crossings have been reported between the Musk Lorikeet and Swainson's Lorikeet.

If kept in the living room they become tame pets and like to romp about on the floor or climb on to the hand or shoulder of their owner.

**Greater Sulphur-crested Cockatoo** (White Cockatoo) *Kakatoe galerita galerita* Pl. 58
*Origin* Australia and Tasmania

18–20 in. *Cock* and *Hen*: Body plumage entirely white with only a yellow suffusion on the ear coverts and on the under tail coverts. The crest is yellow with exception of frontal feathers which are white. Beak black. Eyes are brown-red in the hen and black in the cock, surrounded by a naked orbital ring. Legs a dark grey.

These birds live very well in a strong wire cage or a strongly wired outside aviary. Once they become tame they learn to talk readily and can imitate all manner of sounds and learn tricks.

A large nest box or barrel with some damp wood pulp is necessary. They incubate alternately for about a month; the young will leave the nest after a further 2 months and then soon start feeding themselves. During the rearing of the young, large quantities of hard-boiled egg should be supplied,

together with stale white bread. The normal diet should be varied with green vegetables, fruit, even boiled fish and potatoes. Breeding results were reported in Algiers, Germany and Britain in 1879, 1883, and 1915. A crossing with the Roseate Cockatoo was also successful. These birds may attain a ripe old age. Bad treatment or teasing is never forgotten; they will then become nervous and spiteful and will bite, inflicting a severe wound.

In addition to words and whistling which they have been taught they can, when provoked, screech and yell in most unpleasant fashion. When nesting they lose all confidence, even in those who look after them. They will approach everyone with a great show of aggression, and success may only be looked for if they are left absolutely in peace and undisturbed.

**Lesser Sulphur-crested Cockatoo** *Kakatoe sulphurea sulphurea* Pl. 57
*Origin* Celebes

About 14 in. *Cock:* White with a yellowish tinge; cheek patches yellow; long, curved crest citron yellow; under surface of wings and tail yellow. Irides almost black; legs and feet blackish-grey. *Hen:* Similar but slightly smaller and the eyes reddish-brown.

The most frequently kept of the cockatoos. As a cage bird it is readily tamed and soon grows affectionate.

With children and strangers these small cockatoos are always friendly and seldom attempt to bite. They can be taught all manner of little tricks and their talking ability is second to none. They can also be kept in pairs in an aviary, where they can even spend the winter if adequate shelter is provided.

They have been successfully bred; the 2 or 3 eggs are laid in a large nest box or a roomy hollow log in which there should be a thick layer of wood chips and sawdust. After a month of incubation shared by both birds, the young hatch and remain in the nest for 2 months. They are fully feathered when they leave. The older birds will continue to feed the young for a considerable period. The first breeding result was recorded in Britain in 1922. A cross with the Roseate Cockatoo was also a success.

As rearing food, soaked bread and hard-boiled egg should be given, of which the birds will consume a considerable amount. As they live to a ripe old age and success cannot be looked for until they are fully matured, it may be some years before they will even start to nest. During the nesting season they lose all interest in human society and, in fact, resent interference even from their owner. It is best to leave them entirely to their own devices.

As well as oats, maize, sunflower, millet, canary seed and various nuts, they like carrots and fruit.

The cage must be able to withstand their onslaughts; thick timbers are not proof against their beaks. A very substantial nest box should be provided. Even this will usually be badly chewed.

**Great White Cockatoo** (White-crested Cockatoo, Umbrella Cockatoo) *Kakatoe alba.* Pl. 56
*Origin* The Mollucas
19 in. *Cock:* Entirely white with a sulphur-yellow tinge at the base of the inner webs of flight and tail feathers; crest large, rounded and white. Naked orbital skin bluish; irides almost black; beak and feet black. *Hen:* Similar but the irides warm brown and the beak less massive. The habits and requirements of this bird are the same as for the Salmon-crested Cockatoo which it closely resembles. It is seldom available and the few that are offered by the trade are usually bought and kept in cages as pets. There is, therefore, very little information as to breeding in captivity but there is a record of hybrids between this species and Leadbeater's Cockatoo being reared by birds which were kept at liberty in a park in England.

As a pet, it becomes delightfully tame and affectionate. In spite of its size and massive beak, it is usually extremely gentle and is a talented talker and mimic.

**Salmon-crested Cockatoo** (Rose-crested Cockatoo) (Moluccan Cockatoo) *Kakatoe moluccensis*
*Origin* Moluccas, Amboyna, Ceram
20 in. *Cock:* White with a salmon-coloured suffusion on breast. Crest broad, long and white, only the central feathers being salmon-red. Eyes black, beak black. *Hens* may be recognized by a dark brown iris.

One of the best talkers of the cockatoo tribe, these birds should be given a very large cage and regular exercise and freedom. A real disadvantage is their screeching, which they sometimes keep up for a considerable time. On the other hand, their tameness and affection are really touching.

They are veritable destroyers of wood and they like to gnaw on fresh branches and if provided with the opportunity to do so this will temper their ravages on perches. Their dangerous large beaks are seldom misused once they become accustomed to being well looked after. It is important to obtain a young bird, which will be found very playful, and anxious to be petted and made a fuss of. As a rule these cockatoos are imported at an early age and will have already picked up a word or two. When a choice is offered, a quiet bird should be secured and screechers left severely alone. This habit of screeching can never be cured!

Their care, feeding and maintenance should be the same as other cockatoos.

**Bare-eyed Cockatoo** (Little Corella, Blood-stained Cockatoo, Blue-eyed Cockatoo) *Kakatoe sanguinea sanguinea* Pl. 61
*Origin* Australia generally, but chiefly the inland areas.

14½ in. *Cock:* General colour white, feathers of the lores and head rose-red at the base. Inner webs of the primaries and of all but the central pair of tail feathers sulphur-yellow. Bare patches round eyes dark bluish-grey; irides blackish-brown; beak greyish-horn, legs and feet grey. *Hen:* Similar.

This species is fairly plentiful in Australia and flocks of many thousands are sometimes seen. It normally feeds on the ground, chiefly on the seeds of various grasses, on plants, roots and bulbs. The site chosen for nesting is a hole in the giant gum trees, usually near water, and the clutch normally consists of three pure white eggs.

It is a hardy species and provided it has access to a frost-proof shelter can remain in an outdoor aviary throughout the year. A good-sized nest box or hollow tree trunk should be available at all seasons as these birds often choose to roost in holes rather than on the perches.

Their food should consist of a mixture of canary seed, millet, clipped oats, sunflower seed and a few peanuts. Raw vegetables such as carrots or swedes and raw apple should also be supplied, together with greenstuff, and a fresh turf placed on the ground will provide the birds with the opportunity to exercise their digging propensities.

It bred in the London Zoo in 1907.

**Leadbeater's Cockatoo** (Major Mitchell's Cockatoo, Pink Cockatoo) *Kakatoe leadbeateri leadbeateri* Pl. 63
*Origin* South and interior of Australia

16–17 in. *Cock:* White flushed with pink on the sides of the head, neck, breast and abdomen, the colour being strongest beneath the wings and at the base of the tail; the feathers of the forehead are also rosy-pink at the base and this is particularly noticeable when the crest is raised. The crest is long and pointed, deep orange-vermilion, with a central band of yellow and the tips of the feathers white. Irides almost black; beak pale yellowish; legs and feet blackish-grey. *Hen:* Similar but the irides warm brown. Young birds of both sexes have blackish eyes and at this stage it is almost impossible to sex them. The colour changes slowly in young hens and it may be a full year or more before the change is completed. Subdivision of this species is no longer considered to be justifiable.

On first arrival the birds are usually extremely nervous – and are not easily tamed – but their beautiful colouring compensates for the extra trouble and care necessary to accustom them to their new surroundings. Once their confidence has been won they will soon learn to talk prettily or to whistle.

In their natural state they live largely on the ground where they hunt for grass seeds.

Leadbeater's Cockatoo has been

frequently bred in Britain, and a crossing with a Greater Sulphur-crested Cockatoo and the Roseate Cockatoo seems to have been successful. First results were in Britain in 1901.

Their nesting requirements are similar to those for the Roseate Cockatoo. The cock assists in incubation during the day, the hen remaining on the nest throughout the night. The young are reared largely on green food and fruit, together with regurgitated seed. They mature slowly and remain in the nest for a very long period. The clutch consists of 3–4 eggs. Young birds take about 4 years to fully mature before they commence to breed.

Diet consists of sunflower seed, corn-on-the-cob, ground nuts, canary seed, oats, hemp, much green food, carrots, fruit, white bread and so on.

They need not be kept indoors during the winter if a well-sheltered aviary with a roofed-in partition is available. If kept in a cage they must be given an opportunity to fly about for some time each day.

**Roseate Cockatoo** (Galah, Rose-breasted Cockatoo) *Kakatoe roseicapilla roseicapilla* Pl. 62
*Origin* Australia

14 in. *Cock:* General colour above silvery grey, lighter on the rump; outer webs of the wing coverts and secondaries, crown, hind neck and feathers below the eyes rose tinted white; throat, cheeks, breast, abdomen, and under wing-coverts deep rose-red; flanks and under tail-coverts light grey. Naked skin round eyes dull red; irides dull orange, beak greenish white; legs and feet grey. *Hen:* Similar but irides lighter in colour (according to one authority the eyes of the cock

are very dark, almost black). Immature birds have the feathers of the head and breast grey with only the base of the feathers dull rosy-red.

An albino form is sometimes seen in Australia and has been bred in England. The grey plumage is replaced by white but the rose-coloured breast is retained.

Unless a young bird can be obtained any attempt to keep this beautiful little cockatoo as a cage-bird in the room may prove disappointing, because it is quite exceptional for adult birds to become tame and friendly. Young birds taken from the nest and hand-reared are quite a different story. They are accustomed to human contact from infancy and become the most charming pets. They learn all manner of tricks, allow themselves to be petted, and soon talk amusingly. Like the Sulphur Crested Cockatoos they enjoy a bath and appreciate being sprayed.

Breeding results have been obtained repeatedly, the first time in Britain in 1910. They have also been successfully crossed with Leadbeater's and the Lesser Sulphur-crested Cockatoo.

They are passionately fond of rock salt.

If kept in an outside aviary covered with strong wire-netting, they should be given a good hollow tree trunk into which they can retire for shelter and which will also provide them with ample opportunity to chew.

Only cockatoos kept in the house will become completely tame; so much so that they can be allowed to fly at liberty. They are practically certain to return and during a shower they love to sit amid the dripping wet leaves of a tree and twirl round and round until they become thoroughly soaked.

Food requirements similar to those

of the Lesser Sulphur-crested Cockatoo.

**Cockatiel** *Nymphicus hollandicus*
*Origin* Australia Pl. 64

12 in. *Cock:* General colour greyish-brown, silver-grey on the rump and upper tail coverts; wings dark grey, blackish towards the tips and the primary coverts almost black, an oblong white patch down the centre of the wing; tail, central pair of feathers grey, remainder blackish-brown, some pale grey on the outer webs. Crown, long pointed crest and sides of head lemon-yellow with orange on the ear coverts; nape brownish-grey. Eyes brown, beak dark grey; legs and feet blackish-grey. *Hen:* Duller in colour, head and crest brown washed with yellow and the ear coverts dull orange-red. Narrow yellowish transverse bars on grey of rump and upper tail coverts. Tail, central pair of feathers greyish-brown speckled with white, the two outermost pairs lemon-yellow mottled and barred with dark brown. Lower abdomen and under tail coverts barred with yellow. Both sexes of immature birds resemble the hen.

The Cockatiel is one of the best-known of the larger parrakeets. It is also among the most tolerant, has a pleasant voice, is graceful and breeds readily. Other good points are that it becomes tame very quickly, and learns to whistle simple tunes. It can even be taught to say a few words if kept in a room away from others of its kind.

It loves to fly and is as fast on the wing as any parrakeet. A large flight is therefore desirable although it is not essential for breeding, as they have often been successfully reared in a large cage.

The best plan is to choose a nesting log with a hole in the side, so placed that the bird sitting on the eggs can look out. This species is easily frightened and the hen will quickly abandon the nest if disturbed by sudden or unusual sounds. But if she can look and see what is happening around her she will probably remain sitting quietly.

These birds like a diet consisting mainly of millet, oats, canary seed and a lot of green stuff. Their greatest delight is to eat privet leaves and they also like to feed these to their young. Soaked seeds and bread mixed with hard-boiled egg and fresh ants' eggs make up their favourite rearing food. The young will sit in the nesting log and rock to-and-fro continually, making a peculiar hissing noise when anyone peeps at them. The cock and hen incubate alternately during the day but the hen will sit all night. The first breeding result was obtained in France during 1850.

For those who, after keeping Budgerigars, wish to start with the larger parrot-like species, the Cockatiel will prove an ideal choice. There may be disappointments, but if the birds are healthy and unrelated results may confidently be expected. New blood should be added to the original stock from time to time by an exchange of birds with another breeder. Cockatiels have already been bred in captivity for so many generations that a definite decline in size and stamina may be noticed. Imported birds are usually the more robust, as is the case with the Bourke's Grass Parrakeet, but owing to the ban on the exportation of all forms of native fauna from Australia, it is difficult to obtain wild caught stock.

A hybrid with the Blue-winged Grass Parrakeet is said to have been produced, and an albino form is now being bred.

Of all the larger parrakeets, this is one of the most suitable species with which to make a start. Not only is it pretty in colouring, but its voice is neither unpleasant nor noisy. It can spend summer and winter in an outside flight, provided a well-covered shelter is available and can be kept together with any small birds as it is extremely gentle and peacable.

## Hyacinthine Macaw *Anodorhynchus hyacinthinus* Pl. 44
*Origin* South America, Central Brazil

Nearly 3 ft. *Cock:* Entirely cobalt-blue with lighter and darker shading, flights and tail black. Orange-yellow ring around eye and round base of lower mandible. Beak and legs black. *Hen:* A little smaller.

These birds soon grow tame and affectionate, but owing to their great size and powerful beaks they are only suitable for a very large specially-made iron cage, or a large, strong aviary. In zoos they are kept on a stand attached by a long chain to one leg. They may remain outside during the summer, but should be brought inside in winter, and under these conditions they will do well and live long, but are hardly suitable for an ordinary fancier. When they are in their natural surroundings, they nest in the banks of rivers, digging a deep hole with their beaks. Spraying with tepid water is essential for all parrots if bathing facilities are not available. A sand bath would also be welcome in a large cage.

As well as the parrot mixture of seeds, they should be given green food, nuts, fresh branches, and such-like.

Like all parrots, these Macaws like to sunbathe, but it is wrong to place a cage in a position which offers no opportunity for the bird to retire into the shade when it wishes to do so. It must be remembered that these birds live in tropical forests where there is always ample shade, and they are not accustomed to long exposure to the full heat of the sun.

## Lear's Macaw *Anodorhynchus leari* Pl. 46
*Origin* Brazil

About 30 in. *Cock:* Cobalt blue, back and wing coverts with pale edges to the feathers; head, neck and under parts greenish-blue, the feathers of the abdomen with blue edges. Flights blackish; under surface of tail black. Naked orbital ring orange-yellow and a large patch at base of lower mandible yellow. Eyes brown, beak, legs and feet black. *Hen:* Similar but smaller and with less robust beak. This species closely resembles the Hyacinthine Macaw but is a little smaller and the blue of the plumage is less intense. It requires the same food and treatment.

## Blue and Yellow Macaw *Ara ararauna* Pl. 50
*Origin* South America, Panama to Bolivia and Guiana and throughout the Amazon Valley

34 in. *Cock:* Upper parts blue, the forehead, crown and rump with greenish tone; flights and tail purplish-indigo. Under parts deep yellow; under tail coverts greenish-blue; under side of tail and wings yellow. Naked facial patch greyish-white lined with tiny black feathers and a broad black band extending from the ear coverts round the throat. Eyes pale yellow; beak black; legs and feet dark grey. *Hen:* Slightly smaller with smaller beak.

This specie is regularly offered fors sale, and is an even better talker than the other Macaws. It is, therefore, seldom kept in pairs. Breeding results were obtained in France in 1818.

The care and breeding are as described for the Red and Yellow Macaw. Hybrids are known between this species and the Red and Yellow Macaw and *vice versa*.

**Military Macaw** (Great Green Macaw) *Ara militaris militaris.*
*Origin* South America.

26 in. *Cock:* Red forehead, green crown, olive-green back, blue upper tail coverts and rump, blue and red tail, olive-green under parts with blue under tail coverts, flights green and blue, bare cheek patches flesh-coloured with rows of small violet-brown feathers. Beak black, legs brown-blue, eyes yellow-grey. *Hen:* Is similar in colouring to the cock, but is a trifle smaller and it is very difficult to select a pair.

The Military Macaw is soon tamed and will repeat a few words. It is rather too big for a cage and is better kept in a large indoor or outside aviary. It must, however, be housed in a warm room during the winter. Breeding results have not yet been reported, but there have been crossings with the Red and Yellow Macaw.

Although this Macaw can make an atrocious noise when excited, fortunately it does not give voice to its feelings very often if kept as a pet indoors. It will do well on a parrot stand, better than in a cage. Its enormous beak will soon destroy a perch, necessitating frequent replacement. The bird will be less destructive if given a regular supply of fresh twigs and pieces of wood to play with.

Nuts, soaked maize, carrots, rusks and cake now and again should be provided as well as the normal mixture of parrot seed. Green food should never be lacking.

In their natural state these Macaws use holes in the trunks of trees for nesting.

**Red and Yellow Macaw** (Scarlet Macaw) *Ara macao* Pl. 45
*Origin* South America, South Mexico to the Amazon and Bolivia.

36 in. *Cock:* Scarlet; wing coverts yellow tipped with green, flights blue; rump, upper and under tail coverts blue; tail, two central feathers scarlet tipped with blue, the blue increasing on the other feathers, the outermost being almost entirely blue. Naked skin of cheeks flesh coloured with rows of tiny black feathers. Eyes yellowish-white; beak, upper mandible whitish tipped with black, lower mandible black; legs and feet blackish. *Hen:* Similar but usually a little smaller and with smaller beak.

The Scarlet Macaw is among the most popular of pet birds, not only for its magnificent colouring but also for its attachment to those who care for it. The ability of the bird to learn to speak clearly and its hardiness have made it a popular pet.

These birds are expensive and are seldom kept in pairs, although some breeding results have been obtained. But for talking purposes keeping a pair is invariably unsatisfactory, since a bird which can hear the calls of its own kind will seldom attempt to mimic other sound.

Breeding has succeeded in a large cage as well as in a bird-room, where the pair had been kept on their own. A breeding box of more than 20 in. in diameter is necessary and a crate can be used for this. A thick layer of sawdust should be put inside. The eggs take 25 days to hatch and the young only make an appearance after 3 months in the nest. The birds take 6 months to get their full colouring. The first breeding results were recorded in Britain in 1916. The birds can live to a great age, provided they are well looked after and are not exposed to all the vagaries of our climate.

In addition to the various grains, diet should consist of fruit and green foods in adequate quantities, and all manner of nuts, soaked maize, dry biscuits and rusks. Now and again some boiled rice should be given, also fresh twigs. The perches should be renewed regularly as they are gnawed to pieces by the birds.

The cages should be strong and roomy. Cleaning must be attended to punctiliously if the birds are to be kept in good health. Hybrids have been reported with a Blue and Yellow Macaw.

**Red and Blue Macaw** (Crimson Macaw, Green-winged Macaw) *Ara chloroptera* Pl. 49
*Origin* South America, Guiana and Bolivia

32 in. *Cock:* Deep crimson, rump, upper and under tail coverts pale blue; wings, lesser coverts crimson, median coverts dark green, greater coverts blue, flights blue; tail, two middle feathers deep red tipped with blue, next two pairs blue with red edges towards the base, remainder almost entirely blue, under side of all feathers golden-red. Naked skin on face flesh-coloured, lined with tiny red feathers; eyes straw-yellow; beak, upper mandible horn-white, black at base, lower mandible black; legs and feet greyish-black.

*Hen:* Similar but with shorter and broader beak.

This species has often been confused with the preceding species.

Breeding results have been obtained repeatedly as well as crossings with other macaws.

**Severe Macaw** *Ara severa severa* Pl. 48
*Origin* South America, Panama and Brazil

20 in. *Cock:* Almost entirely green, a little more blue on the head. A brown band and red spot run across forehead, chin and cheek. Wings blue and green, tail green with blue tip. Eyes yellow, beak black, legs brown black. The cheeks are bare and flesh-coloured with a few tiny black feathers. *Hen:* Has a slightly less distinct red spot on the forehead.

These macaws are suitable for a large cage, although they must be allowed frequent exercise outside, either on a stand or on top of the cage.

It is very difficult to select a true pair on account of the similarity of plumage, but, if obtained, the birds may well be kept in a small aviary which must be of sturdy construction. A single bird soon becomes tame and learns to repeat a few words, although not too clearly.

In a breeding-box of some 16 in. by 16 in., with a circular entrance of 6 in in diameter, 2 or 3 eggs will be laid and hatched in 28 days. A layer of damp soil must be placed on the bottom of the nesting-box and a few handfuls of moss on top of the soil; this will prevent the eggs from becoming too dry. The youngsters leave the nest when 7 weeks old. Diet the same as for other Macaws though they can be given for a change soaked maize, some ground nuts, or other small nuts, carrots, green food,

H

cake and biscuits and especially fresh twigs and fruit. Carrots and dandelion buds are a treat. The cock roosts in the nest box during the breeding season. Suitable rearing food is boiled rice and egg food, and bread and milk sweetened with sugar or honey. The youngsters become quite independent after 6 weeks.

**Spix Macaw** *Ara spixii*
*Origin* South America, Eastern Brazil

22 in. *Cock:* pale blue, greyer on the head. Under tail coverts black, beak black, cere grey, eyes white and yellow, legs black. *Hen:* A little smaller and with narrower and smaller beak.

This species is seldom imported and is very expensive. Its keeping and care should be similar to that for the Severe Macaw. It will learn to say a few words, soon grows quite tame and screeches but seldom. Its large beak is never misused. Special parrot accommodation with plenty of room to exercise is very desirable. Spix Macaw has not yet been successfully bred in captivity.

**Illiger's Macaw** *Ara maracana* Pl. 47
*Origin* South America, South Brazil and Paraguay

17 in. *Cock:* Upper parts olive-green, head bluer, forehead red; a red patch on lower back and also on belly. Remainder under parts green. Wings blue and green, tail blue. Eyes red-brown, cheeks and cere yellow, legs dark flesh-coloured, beak brown-black. *Hen:* Smaller and the red on forehead is less well-defined.

These birds do well in a large parrot cage, become tame very quickly and learn to play and talk. They must be let out of the cage daily for exercise, to clamber about and play. They love to be stroked and petted and are affec-

tionate but sometimes lose their temper and will then bite and snap. Breeding results have been obtained repeatedly in roomy surroundings. The nest box should be not less than 14 in. by 16 in. in size. Two eggs will be laid to a clutch and incubation takes 24 days.

The first breeding results were recorded in Germany in 1881 and in Britain in 1931.

The diet should be the same as that given to the Severe Macaw. Fruit is greatly liked. In their natural surroundings these birds are found in great flocks when not breeding.

**Noble Macaw** *Ara nobilis cumanensis*
Pl. 51
*Origin* South America, Brazil

12–12½ in. *Cock:* Green, more yellowish below. Forehead and stripe above the eyes blue; outer webs of flights blue, bend of wings scarlet, underside of wing golden-olive and scarlet; under side of tail also golden-olive. Small, naked orbital patch white; irides yellow; beak, upper mandible horn-white with black tip, lower mandible brownish-black; legs and feet brownish-black. *Hen:* Similar and hard to distinguish from cock but may be slightly smaller.

This is the smallest of the macaws and one which will usually become very tame and gentle. Although it has been known as a cage and aviary bird since 1879, when it was first imported to Berlin, it was not until 1951 that it was first successfully bred, by Mr E. N. T. Vane, in England.

Feeding and treatment should be as described for the Severe Macaw. It has proved to be reasonably hardy when once acclimatized but needs protection during the winter months when it is best accommodated in a heated room.

**Red-headed Conure** *Aratinga erythrogenys* Pl. 68
*Origin* Colombia, Peru and Ecuador

Nearly 16 in. *Cock:* Forehead to centre of crown scarlet, as also face, lores, and chin, lesser under wing coverts, wing edges and thighs. Remainder of plumage entirely green. Sometimes purple feathers in the wings. Eyes yellow, beak pale horn-coloured. Legs brown. *Hen* is similar to cock but a little smaller.

These birds belong to what may be called 'the eager to learn' types which, if kept by themselves, soon become tame and learn to say a few words or sentences. They like to be petted and are therefore quite happy if kept in a cage in the house. Now and again, however, they will suddenly screech, a habit they never seem to lose entirely. They allow themselves to be carried around the house, seated on a friendly shoulder, and they will scramble up and down stairs. Apples and raw root vegetables are usually liked as well as the normal seed mixture for large parrakeets and parrots. Rice is also appreciated. Breeding results are unknown, probably due to the difficulty of selecting a true pair since cock and hen are like peas in a pod. They may winter in frost-proof accommodation, which suits them better than a heated living-room.

**Yellow-headed Conure** (Jenday Conure) *Aratinga jandaya* Pl. 71
*Origin* Eastern Brazil

12 in. *Cock* and *Hen* alike, the latter a little smaller. Head and neck bright yellow suffused with orange-red on forehead, throat and round the eyes; back green, lower back orange-red; wings, coverts green, remainder blue,

the flights with base of feathers green on outer webs; tail, above blue merging into olive-green at base, black below; under parts orange-yellow. eyes pearl-grey to brown; beak, legs and feet blackish.

This bird is peaceable even with others of the same species and several can safely be kept together in a roomy flight. Given treatment as described for Red-headed Conures, they will soon settle down to breed. They sit alternately on the 3 or 4 eggs and drive all intruders away from the vicinity of their nest with a show of ferocity, fluffing up their neck feathers, and making all kinds of nodding movements.

Again, like the previous species, these birds are not too noisy and soon get acclimatized; they breed reasonably well, provided a true pair has been obtained, and will be ornaments to the flight for many a year. The first breeding result was recorded in 1891.

**St Thomas' Conure** *Aratinga pertinax pertinax.*
*Origin* Island of St Thomas, Santa Cruz

10½ in. *Cock:* Has a yellow forehead, yellow chin and sides of head, the crown being bluish. Upper parts entirely green. A brown-grey throat merges into orange-yellow on the breast. Flights are green and blue with black tips. Tail green with a blue tip. Beak black with a white edge, eyes and legs brown. *Hen* is smaller than cock and somewhat duller in colour. In spite of these differences, it is often difficult to select a true pair as different colour forms exist and two birds always act as though they were mates, irrespective of their sex.

They soon become tame and will accept sunflower seeds from the hand.

Some birds will even learn to say a few words. The screeching which they make when frightened can be piercing, but the more the birds grow accustomed to their surroundings, the less it is heard. It is safe to keep them with other birds provided there is sufficient room. As they are not very quick, most other birds are able to seek safety in flight.

Soaked bread and hard-boiled egg are suitable as rearing food, once the pair has decided to start breeding. The hen alone incubates and is fed by the cock. Fresh twigs to chew should always be supplied. The birds are also very fond of green stuff, of which they will eat quantities. Fruit and corn-on-the-cob are acceptable tit-bits.

The first breeding results were recorded in 1949 in America.

**Brown-throated Conure** *Aratinga pertinax aeruginosa* Pl. 70
*Origin* Guiana, Venezuela and Rio Negro
About 9¾ in. *Cock* and *Hen* alike but hen slightly smaller. Above green with blue tinge on crown of head. Forehead, cheeks, ear coverts and throat brown; breast, abdomen and under tail-coverts greenish-yellow with orange-yellow in middle of abdomen. Flights blue and tail green with blue at tips of central feathers. Eyes golden-brown with naked orbital ring orange-yellow; beak horn-brown; legs and feet brown.

This is closely related to above and bred for the first time in England during 1908.

**Yellow-cheeked Conure** (Guiana Brown-throated Conure) *Aratinga pertinax chrysophrys*
*Origin* Southern British Guiana

10 in. *Cock* and *Hen* exactly alike, and it is extremely difficult to pick a true pair.

Very similar to the Brown-throated Conure, *A.p. aeruginosa*, but with more distinct yellow orbital ring, yellower on the cheeks and greener on abdomen.

Like lovebirds, they will sit on a perch in couples, but this is not evidence that they are a pair, and it is only by purchasing a number and keeping them together that a cock and hen may eventually prove their sex.

Together with other larger parrakeets in an outside aviary, one pair took possession of a hollow log which had been fixed in a quiet spot with its entrance to the north. The bottom had been covered with a layer of damp soil over which some handfuls of moss had been placed. A clutch of 4 eggs were laid, one egg every day. The hen incubated and was joined by the cock during the night. It was 26 days before the first egg hatched and a further 6 weeks before the first youngster left the nest to be followed two days after by another two.

White bread and milk, much apple and green food, and the normal seed menu for the large parrakeets, formed the ordinary diet during and before the breeding season.

It does not seem possible to keep these birds in colonies like Lovebirds, for they are apt to fight, and this usually results in the death of one or more birds. They can, however, be associated with a pair of parrakeets of another species, a pair of lovebirds, or other large birds with comparative safety.

As with all other parrots, frost-bitten toes must be guarded against during the winter. They should then be confined to a frost-proof shelter at night but may be allowed to use the open flight during the day.

## Cactus Conure *Aratinga cactorum cactorum* Pl. 65
*Origin* Brazil

10¼ in. *Cock:* Green above, forehead grey-brown, crown blue-grey. Side of head and throat grey-brown. Breast and abdomen orange-yellow. Beak horn-coloured. Legs grey. *Hen:* Duller in colouring.

Soon tamed in captivity, these birds allow themselves to become pets. Their voice is not too penetrating, and not even disturbing in the house. They will eat an ordinary seed diet suitable for parrakeets, also sunflower seed and oats. Green food and fruit, especially apples, should not be omitted.

Although I have owned a pair for some time, they have not yet started preparations for breeding. They are mutually sympathetic but the cock seems to feel drawn to an Indian Ring-necked Parrakeet, which does not disdain his advances.

Breeding results were reported for the first time in the United Kingdom in 1914 and again in 1927.

## Golden-crowned Conure *Aratinga aurea aurea* Pl. 66
*Origin* Brazil.

11¼ in. *Cock:* Large orange-yellow spot from forehead to the centre of the head followed by blue on the crown; lores blue; orbital ring orange. Upper parts green, cheeks, neck and breast olive-green; under parts yellow-green. Wings green and blue with black tips. Tail green with a blue tip. Eye orange, cere grey; beak and legs dark grey. *Hen:* Similar to Cock but has somewhat paler colouring.

Kept alone in a cage, one of these birds will soon grow tame; it will learn, if it is a young bird, to whistle tunes and repeat words.

These birds are hardy and can winter in frost-proof accommodation; their shrieking is neither prolonged nor disturbing. Breeding results have been obtained repeatedly, even in a cage in which a nest box of 10 in. by 12 in. had been fixed, with an entrance of 3 in. diameter. Incubation lasts 26 days, and the young remain in the nest for about 50 days. Two clutches are sometimes laid in succession. The hen and cock take turns at incubating.

The first breeding results were reported from Germany in 1880.

A pair can be kept in a small aviary by themselves, but they have also bred in an enclosure shared with Cactus Conures, *Aratinga cactorum.* As a general rule, however, the cock will attack all other parrakeets during the breeding time.

## Black-headed Conure
(Nanday Conure) *Nandayus nenday* Pl. 67
*Origin* South America, Paraguay

About 12 in. *Cock:* Upper parts grass-green; forehead, crown and front of cheeks black, back of head dark brown; ear coverts, rump and abdomen yellowish-green; throat and upper breast greyish blue-green; flights, secondaries and primary coverts blue, the latter edged with yellowish-green; tail olive-green tipped blue; thighs red; eyes are dark brown, legs and feet dark grey with black claws; beak blackish. *Hen:* Similar but slightly smaller.

This species has been frequently imported in the past and can be kept with other nearly-related species in a roomy flight. After a short time they become accustomed to their owner and lose their first extreme wildness. They will breed in captivity if a large nesting box is made available and hung in such a way that they can sit on top of it.

Variety of food, plenty of green stuff, fruit and fresh twigs are indispensable. Half-ripe grain such as wheat, oats, rye, and maize are necessary during nesting and also soaked stale bread, rock salt and lime.

They are cheerful birds, keeping together in pairs, are not too noisy and become quite hardy when once acclimatized. They are therefore able to winter outside, provided a draught-proof shelter is available.

The first breeding results were obtained in the United Kingdom in 1901 and in France in 1881. A hybrid with the Yellow-headed Conure was produced in 1951.

**Brown-eared Conure** (Red-bellied Conure) *Pyrrhura frontalis frontalis*
*Origin* Brazil and Paraguay

Nearly 11 in. *Cock:* Upper parts dark grass-green, band across forehead red-brown, ear coverts brown-yellow, wings green and blue, centre of abdomen red, eye brown, beak dark grey, legs grey-black. *Cock* and *Hen* difficult to distinguish so not easy to secure a true pair. The Brown-eared Conure, though shy at first, very quickly becomes accustomed to its new surroundings if it is housed in a large aviary with other large parrakeets. Later on it can be gradually accustomed to a cage if desired. It will become quite a pet.

A pair bred for the first time in the United Kingdom in 1924, and it has been successfully crossed with the White-eared Conure, *Pyrrhura leucotis*.

**White-eared Conure** *Pyrrhura leucotis leucotis* Pl. 69
*Origin* Eastern Brazil

8¼ in. *Cock* and *Hen* practically alike: green above with a red-brown rump. Head dark brown, ear coverts grey-white. Forehead and cheek stripes red-brown. Nape and throat blue. Breast green with black and white horizontal stripes. Abdomen green with a red-brown spot. Wings green and blue. Tail red-brown. Eyes orange-brown with a white orbital ring. Beak and legs black.

Kept as a pair in an outside flight they show up most favourably and may start breeding. A nest box 8 in. by 12. in., with an entrance hole 2½ in. in diameter, or hollow log is necessary. The two eggs are incubated solely by the hen. Corn-on-the-cob and sunflower seed are a treat. Oats and hemp should form part of the ordinary diet. Many fresh twigs and young foliage, as well as powdered egg shells, boiled potatoes, carrots, boiled maize and soaked stale bread, will give the varied diet needed.

The birds readily become acclimatized and may even winter outside if care is taken that they have a draught-proof and damp-proof shelter.

Breeding results were reported from Austria as far back as 1880. Hybrids with a Brown-eared Conure have been obtained.

**Quaker Parrakeet** (Grey-breasted Parrakeet) *Myiopsitta monachus monachus*
*Origin* South America, Argentina, Paraguay, Uruguay and Bolivia

11½ in. Sexes alike but hen is said to be more robust and to have a much longer and stronger beak. Prevailing colour green, yellower on the under parts; wings green with blue secondaries and flights; forehead, face, throat and breast grey, most of the feathers having very pale margins which convey the impression of scales. Beak dull flesh-colour; eyes dark brown; legs and feet yellowish-grey.

These birds belong to the most interesting of the parrot group since they do not nest in hollow trees but build enormous nests of branches and twigs. For this reason they are more suited to aviary life and their harsh screeching makes them unsuitable as house pets. Lively, active and of sober colouring, they will immediately begin building a nest if a suitable place is available. The more room at their disposal, the larger will be the nest. Usually they make two compartments, one for brooding and one for roosting, while a vaulted entrance serves as a look-out post.

As well as oats, sunflower seed, hemp, corn-on-the-cob, millet and canary seed are eaten, while all kinds of fruit, fresh twigs with young buds, and green stuff must be included in the regular diet. During the nesting period, which usually falls in autumn or winter, soaked bread and hard-boiled egg may be used for the rearing of the young. Once the eggs have been laid and the hen has started incubating, it is quite safe to let them fly at liberty. They will return regularly, and in summer will find most of their food outside. This is not too good for nearby fruit trees, but if only one or two birds fly around, no serious harm will be done. Once the young birds from one or two nests are outside, however, they can cause extensive damage and if the trees which they attack happen to be in a neighbour's garden, there is likely to be trouble.

The birds soon get used to our climate and are absolutely hardy. The only drawback is that the young, even if they are parted from the old birds quite early in life, cannot get out of the habit of screeching. This is why many people, for the sake of living in peace with their neighbours, find it undesirable to keep these birds. A blue variety has been imported from Holland and a hybrid with the Golden-crowned Conure has been reported.

Early breedings were reported in Austria in 1867 and in Germany in 1896.

### Lineolated Parrakeet *Bolborhynchus lineola lineola*

*Origin* Central America

6¾ in. *Cock* and *Hen* alike; the latter is a trifle smaller with less black markings. Head and neck yellowish-green, remainder of upper parts green, all feathers having narrow black margins. Wings green and black, tail green with darker quill stripes. Eye yellow-brown, beak light horn-coloured, legs flesh-coloured.

These little parrakeets are among the most agreeable inhabitants of cage and aviary. Their soft chattering is not disturbing, they are very tolerant with other birds, they settle down quite readily, and if only one is kept, it will soon learn to speak a few words. They live mostly on the ground in the aviary and can run quite fast. They must always have a supply of fresh twigs available, preferably those of apple and pear trees. Millet, canary seed and oats are favourite seeds. They will take pieces of apple and pear when these are offered through the wire netting.

Breeding results have repeatedly been reported since the first success in 1902.

**Passerine Parrotlet** (Guiana Parrotlet)
*Forpus passerinus passerinus*
*Origin* Guiana, Surinam and Cayenne

5½ in. *Cock:* Rich green with yellowish tone on face and under parts and emerald round eye. Lower back, secondaries and wing coverts deep blue. Beak whitish-horn. *Hen:* Entirely green.

These birds are best kept in pairs as they are most affectionate, one to another, and they tolerate the company of other birds quite well except during the breeding season. When breeding, however, they become aggressive and will sometimes bite and break the legs of smaller birds. Their note is like the soft 'chirrup' of a sparrow. It is a fallacy to suggest that these birds would die of loneliness if kept without a mate of their own species. Should one die and the other quickly follow, the cause will probably be found to be due to an infectious disease – not a broken heart! However, if kept by themselves the birds do become dull; they usually sit and mope and only leave their perches to eat and drink. Kept as a pair in a roomy flight, they are sociable and lively; they clamber from perch to perch like the miniature parrots they are. Their emerald-green colour and their activity, together with their soft voices and lack of harsh notes, recommend them as house pets. Experience shows that they need much more care than Budgerigars; they are much more sensitive to damp and cold and require a more varied diet – green stuff and fruit such as apples, pears, berries, plums and so on. Sunflower seed, oats and hemp seed may also be given them, together with canary seed and millet.

Not every pair will become tame. Some will always hide in a corner of the cage as soon as anyone comes to have a look at them. From sheer fright they will make a most unpleasant screeching or croaking noise. Birds bred in this country generally grow out of their shyness and become the jolliest of indoor pets. They should not be allowed to winter outside as they are more susceptible to our damp weather than to cold.

In a cage or aviary they will soon begin to breed. For nesting they use a nest box or hollow log and lay 4–9 eggs on which they will sit for 20 days. After more than a month the young will appear; they will need feeding for a few more months by the parents, after which they must be separated. Stale soaked bread may be given to the adults when rearing young. Fresh twigs and branches must be regularly supplied to satisfy their desire for gnawing. This keeps their beaks from over-growing, and there is also food value in the sap and green wood. The hen only will incubate and the cock will usually remain sitting near the nest; he will feed the hen regularly, as well as the young.

This species was first imported by Germany in 1882, and by Britain in 1926.

**Venezuelan Green-rumped Parrotlet** *Forpus passerinus viridissimus*
*Origin* South America – Guiana, Venezuela

5 in. *Cock:* Almost entirely green, only the innermost wing coverts being blue above and below. *Hen:* Easily distinguished as she is entirely green, lacking the blue on the wings.

This, and the following species, require exactly the same treatment as that described for the Passerine Parrotlet.

**Blue-rumped Parrotlet** (Turquoise-rumped or Mexican Parrotlet) *Forpus cyanopygius cyanopygius*
*Origin* Tres Marias Islands off west coast of Mexico

5 in. *Cock:* Similar to the Passerine Parrotlet, except that the blue areas are turquoise. *Hen:* Entirely green.

**White-winged Parrakeet** *Brotogeris versicolurus versicolurus* Pl. 74
*Origin* Amazon Valley

8¾ in. Sexes alike. Deep grass green above, yellowish-green below; forehead, lores and upper part of cheeks bluish-grey; outer flight feathers black with outer web and tip blue, three succeeding flights blue with green outer edge, remaining flights and secondaries white, the latter with slight yellowish tone; greater wing coverts yellow; eyes brown, beak pale horn-coloured; legs and feet brownish-flesh.

Their maintenance presents no difficulties. A normal diet should be given as for others of the genus with the addition of bread and milk; green food and fruit should figure on the menu. It is difficult to select a pair, but from a number of birds it should be possible with a little trouble to get a cock and hen.

**Canary-winged Parrakeet** *Brotogeris versicolurus chiriri* Pl. 72
*Origin* S. E. Brazil and Bolivia

9½ in. *Cock* and *Hen* alike: Entirely green, under parts lighter. Primary coverts yellow, tail blue below. Eye brown. Beak horn-coloured. Legs flesh-coloured.

Although the voice of these birds is rather loud and screeching, they have many good qualities, such as their extraordinary tameness and their endearing ways. A bird kept singly may become a favourite pet, and will learn to say a few words. A nest box with a layer of damp soil and a layer of moss should be hung high up with the entrance facing north.

The birds are able to stand our climate provided an adequate shelter is attached to the aviary, and can safely spend the winter outside. They bred for the first time in America in 1930.

**Tovi Parrakeet** *Brotogeris jugularis jugularis*
*Origin* Colombia and Central America

7½ in. *Cock* and *Hen* alike, but the cock usually larger. Green, orange spot on chin, wings green and brown with blue on primary coverts, beak horn-coloured, legs flesh-grey.

When first imported, these birds are delicate and need warmth. They must also become accustomed to a seed diet to which fruit (which they eat almost exclusively in their natural state) must be added in liberal quantities.

They like to roost in a hollow log, and this must be available right from the beginning in their new home. They may be timid at first, but later on they become very tame and will probably breed in a large cage or in an aviary. It is preferable to keep them with other birds or with others of their own kind. They are very sociable and like company and should therefore always be kept in pairs. They will learn to speak a word or two.

Boiled maize is a good rearing food for the young, as well as fruit, green food and the normal seed diet.

The first breeding results recorded were from Germany in 1873. A cross between the Tovi Parrakeet, and the White-winged Parrakeet, *Brotogeris ver-*

*sicolurus versicolurus*, has also been reported.

## Golden-fronted Parrakeet (Tuipara)
*Brotogeris chrysopterus tuipara*
*Origin* Brazil

8 in. *Cock* and *Hen* alike. Green, lighter on under parts, head bluish. Narrow stripe of golden-yellow on forehead and a spot on chin. Wing coverts orange. Primaries black-blue with green margins and tips. Eye brown with blue-green orbital ring, beak light horn, legs flesh-coloured.

These parrrakeets are agreeable birds and spend most of their time high up in the aviary. They are slow climbers, and even if they should be inclined to attack other inhabitants of their enclosure, they lack the necessary speed to catch their intended victim, but they would not be safe company for other birds if kept in a small cage. A pair by themselves soon become tame, but their grating voice makes them unpopular as house pets.

They need a seed mixture as used for other parrakeets, much green food, apple, and other fruit; boiled rice and soaked stale bread should be given to provide variety. Fresh twigs from fruit trees or willows should always be supplied.

This species should almost certainly breed in a bird-room or aviary, but details of their breeding habits are not available.

## Tui Parrakeet
*Brotogeris st thoma st thoma* Pl. 73
*Origin* Brazil, the Island of St Thomas

7½ in. *Cock:* Green, rump and under parts lighter green. Forehead yellow and yellow stripe behind eye, some blue in wings. Eye brown, beak light horn-coloured, legs greyish horn-coloured. *Hen:* Similar, but lacks the yellow stripe behind the eye.

As well as a seed mixture, they must have a quantity of fruit and green food. They may be kept together with other birds provided they are not of related species, in a roomy aviary, but they need careful acclimatizing. Their voice is sharp, but not very disturbing. They will grow fairly tame and are best kept in pairs; they usually sit close together, even should they be both of the same sex. With careful attention it should be quite possible to obtain breeding results, and should young be hatched, porridge could be given in addition to soaked maize or bread and milk. A nesting log as used for cockatiels is quite suitable for these small parrakeets.

## Black-headed Caique *Pionites melanocephala melanocephala* Pl. 76
*Origin* South America, Guiana

Nearly 10 in. *Cock* and *Hen* alike: Crown black with green lores, brownish-yellow back. Remainder of upper parts green, throat and under tail coverts yellow. The under parts yellow-white. Wings and tail green. Eye brown, legs brown. Black orbital ring and black beak.

These birds should be cared for in the same way as Amazon parrots. They need much green food and fruit, also nuts and especially maize.

Their loud screeching can be very annoying, but the tamer they grow the less frequently will this noise be made. They can be very amusing, climbing cleverly up the curtain cords, playing on the floor with marbles, which they roll along the floor with their beaks, and tumbling downstairs. But some are inclined to be spiteful and do not hesitate to use their beaks to their owners' discomfort.

The only record of any attempt to breed was between this species and the White-bellied Caïque and occurred in the USA in 1935 and again in Britain in the following year.

As they are so rarely obtainable, this no doubt accounts for the lack of other records. They may be kept in the outside aviary summer and winter, but they must have an adequate shelter which should be heated in severe weather.

**White-bellied Caique** *Pionites leucogaster leucogaster* Pl. 75
*Origin* South America, Lower Amazon

About 10 in. *Cock:* Head and neck brownish-yellow; sides of head, throat and under tail coverts yellow, remainder of under parts white; upper parts, wings and tail green. Eyes brown, with a naked orbital ring which is reddish in colour. Beak horn-coloured, legs brown. *Hen:* Similar.

It requires the same treatment as the Black-headed Caïque (above).

**Blue-headed Parrot** (Red-vented Parrot) *Pionus menstruus* Pl. 83
*Origin* Central and South America.

11½ in. *Cock:* Head and neck dusky blue, ear coverts with a black spot. Remainder green. There is a light red spot on throat, under tail coverts are red with a flecking of blue. Tail blue, eyes brown, eye cere grey. Beak and legs dark grey. *Hen:* Difference between cock and hen is slight. In the hen the blue areas have a greenish tone. It is important to obtain young birds, for an old bird can screech abominably and it is difficult to cure this bad habit. Young birds become very tame and are

then quiet and peaceful and will learn to say a few words.

Breeding results have often been reported; the first was from Britain in 1902. The care of these birds presents no special difficulty; in addition to a good parrot seed mixture they like soaked maize and fruit.

**Cuban Amazon Parrot** (White-headed Amazon Parrot) *Amazona leucocephala leucocephala*
*Origin* Cuba.

Nearly 13 in. *Cock:* Crown, lores and rim around the eyes white, ear coverts black, cheeks and throat rose-pink, belly wine-red in the centre. Remainder green, the feathers having black margins. Blue in the wings and tail. Beak whitish, legs flesh-coloured. *Hen:* Said to be a little smaller than the cock, and to have less pink at the throat and less intense wine-red on the belly.

As young birds all resemble the hen, it is not always easy to select a true pair.

They are among the most beautiful of the Amazons, and combine with other good qualities that of talking well. If acquired young enough, they will become affectionate and gentle. They are, however, less fluent in speech than some of their less beautiful relations. The care needed is exactly the same as that for other Amazons.

Boosey mentions a breeding success in his own aviary. He gave as extra food hemp and white bread and milk sweetened, some boiled potatoes, carrots, spinach leaves and apples. His young birds took four years to mature and reach breeding condition. First breeding result was obtained in Japan in 1922.

The birds are hardy, so long as they have a dry shelter for the night. As they are extremely active, they lend themselves best to an outside aviary and are not very suitable for a cage.

A cross between a Cuban Amazon and a Blue-fronted Amazon was reported many years ago.

**White-fronted Amazon Parrot** (Spectacled Amazon Parrot) *Amazona albifrons albifrons*
*Origin* Central America

Nearly 11 in. *Cock:* Green with a white front, lores and crown blue, orbital ring red. Upper tail coverts yellow-green; vent and a splash on wing red. Tail green with a yellow tip. Eye yellow-white, beak yellow, legs greyish. *Hen:* Red on vent and wings replaced by green.

The talking ability of these birds is rated highly. Kept singly in a large cage, this parrot will certainly become a favourite pet, seldom giving voice to unpleasant screeching. Breeding results have been reported several times; first in the USA in 1949. It has also been crossed with a Green-cheeked Amazon.

Care and feeding should not differ from that for other parrots of this genus.

**Yellow-cheeked Amazon Parrot**
*Amazona autumnalis autumnalis*
*Origin* South America, Mexico

13½ in. *Cock* and *Hen* alike: Crown and neck green, tips of the feathers mauve with black margins. Forehead and lores scarlet. Cheeks golden-yellow with a touch of red. Remainder of the plumage is green. Wings green with some red and blue. Tail green and yellow. Beak horn-coloured, eyes brown; legs grey-green.

Although rather timid and wild at first, these birds accustom themselves quickly to new surroundings. For-

tunately their penetrating screeching is practically never heard; this, of course, adds to their attraction as cage birds, but they do not make very good talkers. By nature they are gentle and affectionate. In an aviary, however, it is advisable only to keep a single pair as they can be very ferocious with their own kind. They are hardy birds and can winter out of doors if their shelter is adequately protected against draughts.

**Festive Amazon Parrot** *Amazona festiva festiva* Pl. 80
*Origin* South America, East Peru

14 in. *Cock:* Forehead and lores plum red, eyebrow stripe and chin blue, lower back and rump red; upper parts green, under parts a trifle lighter green; wings green with black lacing and blue flights. Tail green with yellow tips to feathers. Eyes orange yellow greyish orbital ring. Pale flesh-coloured beak. *Hen:* Similar but usually a little smaller and with smaller head.

These birds are renowned for readily becoming tame and affectionate. But they lack the talent for speech, and this makes them less attractive as cage pets.

They are hardy birds, but warm accommodation is advisable for the winter nights.

**Blue-fronted Amazon Parrot** *Amazona aestiva aestiva* Pl. 77
*Origin* South America, Brazil, Bolivia, Paraguay and Argentina.

About 15 in. Sexes alike but scarlet on shoulder of hen usually less prominent and head smaller. *Cock:* General colour grass green, under parts of a rather lighter shade, forehead blue; crown, side of head and throat yellow; the extent of both the blue and yellow varying greatly in different individuals. Shoulder and third and fourth flight feathers scarlet; first and second flights blue; tail green washed with red on the central feathers. Eyes orange, beak blackish, legs and feet grey.

Their food should consist of buck-wheat, canary seed, sunflower seed, and some barley or oats. Fruit such as oranges, apples, raw carrots, dates and raisins and, of course, all kinds of nuts, can be given as treats.

The birds may sometimes be rather noisy in the early morning but on the whole they are never too bad. They learn to imitate everything, and will talk quite amusingly.

Breeding results were reported in Britain in 1939 and a hybrid with the Green-cheeked Parrot has also been recorded.

A young bird required as a pet should be entirely segregated and only allowed to come into contact with human beings. Such a bird soon becomes tame and will imitate sounds perfectly.

**Yellow-fronted Amazon Parrot** (Yellow-headed Amazon) *Amazona ochrocephala ochrocephala*
*Origin* South America, Venezuela

15½ in. Sexes alike: Dark grass-green on the upper parts with black margins to feathers, lighter towards rump and under parts. Forehead stripe light blue-green, crown lores and chin yellow, and sometimes the yellow extends over whole head. Feathers of neck have black margins. Wings green with red and yellow on shoulders and blue on flights, eyes red, cere bluish white, beak black with a reddish spot on either side, legs blue-grey.

Breeding results have only been achieved with a sub-species the Panama Amazon, *Amazona ochro-cephala panamensis*.

Yellow-fronted Amazons talk well, and can also imitate other sounds excellently; they will laugh, cry, sing and whistle. The natives rate these birds highly and train them carefully, and the most accomplished talkers are seldom allowed to be exported. The ability to learn varies in each bird. In *Parrots,* Boosey describes how a bird which had escaped returned of its own volition to its aviary after a few days' freedom. This bird must have been quite tame and very fond of its owner. A young bird will learn well and quickly if kept by itself in a cage.

**Panama Amazon Parrot** *Amazona ochrocephala panamensis*
*Origin* Panama and Colombia

12 in. Sexes alike: Similar in general appearance to the Yellow-fronted Amazon Parrot but the feathers of the neck are blue-green and lack the black margins. It also has a yellow stripe across the forehead. Beak yellow horn coloured.

This species was bred in the USA in 1945 and a hybrid with the Levaillant's Parrot has been reported. It is known for its ability to talk well, and it will grow tame and affectionate. It is fairly small and is quite suitable for a cage, especially if given its liberty for a time each day to take exercise.

**Yellow-naped Amazon Parrot** *Amazona ochrocephala auro-palliata* Pl. 78
*Origin* Western Central America, Guatemala to Costa Rica and Tigre and Ruatan Islands.

15 in. *Cock* and *Hen* alike. Grass green, rather paler below; the nape yellow, this colour often extending to the crown; edge and bend of the wing with a few red feathers and the speculum also red, flights blackish with the

outer webs green and the tips washed with blue; tail green with a yellowish band and some red at the base of the outer feathers; eyes orange-red; beak horn; legs and feet dusky.

Requires similar feeding and treatment to other Amazons – it is said to be the most talented talker, gentle and affectionate and one of the most desirable of parrots. It was first seen at the London Zoo in 1844.

## Yellow-bellied Senegal Parrot (Yellow-vented Senegal Parrot) *Poicephalus senegalus senegalus*

*Origin* Gambia, West Africa

10½ in. *Cock:* Head, cheeks, ear coverts and throat dark grey, remainder of upper parts green, the flights and tail feathers being brownish-black edged with green on the outer webs; under parts yellow shading to orange in the centre of the belly, and with a green band across the breast; flanks also green; eyes yellow; beak blackish, legs and feet also blackish. *Hen:* Usually has the grey of the head lighter, the under parts are pale yellow lacking the orange tone and the under tail coverts are greenish.

Birds of the group to which this parrot belongs are kept less for their ability to talk than for their graceful appearance. The older cocks especially are beautifully coloured. When the birds are obtained young, there is a good chance that they will grow tame; older birds usually remain timid. As soon as they fear danger, whether real or imagined, they make a most horrible noise.

They like corn on the cob in addition to the usual seed mixture, and all kinds of fruit can form part of their diet.

A pair may probably start nesting and, if a quiet aviary is provided, they should be successful but records of young having been reared are very few indeed. The birds cannot take wing very easily from the ground, unless they have plenty of room, and the aviary should therefore, not be too small. They bathe frequently and thoroughly.

## Orange-bellied Senegal Parrot
(Kano Yellow-vented Senegal Parrot) *Poicephalus senegalus mesotypus* Pl. 79

Very similar to the Yellow-bellied Senegal Parrot, but the under parts are deep orange in colour. There is a further sub-species, the Red-vented or Scarlet-bellied Senegal, *P.s. versteri* which is even deeper in colour.

## Meyer's Parrot (Sudan Brown Parrot) *Poicephalus meyeri meyeri* Pl. 82
*Origin* N.W. Africa

9½ in. *Cock:* Head, back, wings and tail brown and grey, sometimes a yellow stripe over the head; edge and bend of wings, under wing coverts and thighs yellow. Under parts and rump, green to blue-green. Eye orange-red with a very dark cere. Beak, black, legs black-grey. *Hen:* Smaller and has a much less powerful beak.

Like the Senegal Parrot, these small parrots become very tame and playful. They are very suitable as pets as they seldom screech and are very good with children. They live on fruit and seeds of forest trees, so they will thrive best on the seed mixture given to other parrots, with nuts, fruit, such as figs, dates, apples and green food, as extras.

Meyer's Parrot bred for the first time in South Africa in 1952.

## Ruppell's Parrot *Poicephalus ruppellii* Pl. 81
*Origin* South-western Africa from Damaraland to Angola.

9 in. *Cock:* Smokey-brown; sides of head and ear coverts silvery-grey; rump and upper tail coverts dusky brown with darker edges; bend and front edges of wing yellow; under wing coverts and thighs also yellow; eyes orange; beak, legs and feet dark horn-coloured. *Hen:* Smaller and has the rump and upper tail coverts bright blue and the under tail coverts pale dull blue.

Ruppell's Parrot is very similar in habits to Meyer's Parrot and requires similar feeding and treatment.

**African Grey Parrot** *Psittacus erithacus erithacus* Pl. 85
*Origin* Equatorial Africa

About 14 in. *Cock:* With the exception of the tail entirely grey, pale on the rump and belly; tail and under tail coverts bright scarlet. There is a large, naked orbital patch which is whitish flesh-colour; irides cream; legs and feet and also the beak black. *Hen:* Similar in colouring but the head slightly smaller and more rounded and the naked orbital patch rounded instead of obtusely pointed behind as in the cock.

This species was known to the Egyptians, and it is almost certain that it was the first species of parrot ever to be brought to Europe.

It is the most talented of all parrots and gives the impression that not only does it repeat words excellently, but manages to say certain sentences with the right intonation, thus correctly associating sounds with actions. It will talk in a sad, indignant or querulous tone, and will imitate all sounds in masterly fashion.

It is not easy, however, to select a bird which is likely to prove of outstanding ability as the talents of all birds naturally vary. There are those which learn mainly to imitate the whistling of tunes, others which are adept at learning to mimic the human voice, coughing, sneezing, laughing, and those most in demand, of course – the proved good talkers.

Grey Parrots are reputed to live to a great age, even for 80–100 years, and it is understandable that some have become family 'heirlooms' and may speak the language of a bygone age. It sometimes happens that birds have learnt undesirable expressions of which their owner may wish to cure them. This can usually be achieved by placing the bird with another of its own kind, when it will forget the sounds it has learnt to mimic and revert to its own, natural language.

Parrots are often found plucked nearly bare; this is usually due to a fault in their diet. The best remedy is to feed them sunflower seed, canary seed, ground nuts and oats in equal parts. They like to eat remnants of a human meal but should not be given any meat. Fruit and green stuff are essential.

It is rare for this species to breed in captivity, and this may to some extent be due to the difficulty of obtaining a true pair. It has been claimed that the first breeding occurred in 1945, in England but, in fact, a young bird was reared in Germany in 1901. France seems to have claimed breeding results back in 1774 and there is a record of breeding in Britain in 1843.

The hen shows her desire to nest by starting to scratch busily in a corner of the cage. The pair should then be transferred to an indoor aviary which they may have to themselves, and a large hollow log or nest box placed on the floor. The hen will incubate for about a month, and the young will remain in the nest for a further two months.

Rearing food should consist of hardboiled egg, stale white bread, soaked canary seed, boiled maize or boiled potatoes and some hemp.

A good nest can be made of a small beer barrel or cask, the bottom of which has been covered with a layer of peat dust.

According to P. K. Desai of Bhavnager, who breeds these parrots regularly in India with excellent results, young imported birds should be kept together for a considerable time. It will soon be evident which are cocks and which are hens; the former will start feeding first and the hens will 'beg for food' in front of them with their tails spread out.

When the pairs had been selected they were given separate accommodation and in due course 3 to 5 eggs were laid in a native earthenware water jar which had been partly buried in the sand floor. For the first few days the hen feeds the young on a milky substance which has been secreted in her crop.

When a parrot is kept singly, a metal cage should be used, since no wood will resist the onslaught of their beaks. The desire to gnaw should be gratified with thick fresh branches.

On the whole, the cocks are more amenable to learning than the hens.

**Pesquet's Parrot** *Psittrichas fulgidus*
*Origin* New Guinea

About 16 in. *Cock:* Black from head to tail, relieved by a splendid scarlet on wings, belly and under tail coverts. Throat is dusky grey and there is a red spot behind the eye. The large beak is black, eyes brown, and legs dark grey. *Hen:* Similar but lacks the red spot behind the eye.

This is a rare and costly bird and is not very likely to come into the hands of a private collector. Nevertheless, it is worthy of mention in this book.

Its voice is penetrating and shrill, its tail is like a tasselled fan and its head feathers are bushy and brushed up in a 'crew cut'.

These birds feed on bananas and other fruit and are highly appreciated by the natives. In their natural state they are usually met with in pairs only. The Wassenaar Zoo at The Hague has succeeded in keeping a Pesquet's Parrot in good condition.

**African Ring-necked Parrakeet**
*Psittacula krameri krameri*
*Origin* Africa, Senegal to Abyssinia

Similar in all respects to the Indian species except that the beak is blackish or slaty-purplish red and the birds are a little smaller. This species is less frequently available but requires the same treatment as for the Indian Ringnecked Parrakeet, *Psittacula krameri manillensis*

**Alexandrine Parrakeet** *Psittacula eupatria nipalensis* Pl. 87
*Origin* Ceylon, Nepal, Burmah

Up to 20 in. *Cock:* Entirely green; only back of head and cheeks have a grey-blue haze. A black line runs from the nostrils to eye, while lower sides of the cheeks show a black stripe, running to the lower mandible. Neck band is pink. Tail has green-blue feathers with yellow tips. Eye grey with red eyelids. Beak blood-red. Legs grey. *Hen:* Lacks the black facial markings and the pink neckband.

There are several races which show only slight variation.

This species is imported less frequently than the Indian Ring-necked Parrakeet, and is less well liked. It is kept alone in a cage for its talking ability. A pair should also be kept by themselves in an aviary, as usually they are far less tolerant than the Indian Ring-necked, although their care and treatment should be exactly similar. The nest box, however, must be considerably larger. The first breeding results in Europe were recorded in 1899. These birds are hardy and can always be kept outside but should have some protection on frosty nights.

Crossing with the Indian Ring-necked Parrakeet has proved successful. A blue variety appeared in India in 1923 as well as a lutino, and both mutations were subsequently bred in Britain.

**Indian Ring-necked Parrakeet** *Psittacula krameri manillensis* Pl. 84
*Origin* India, Ceylon and Indo-Burmese region to Cochin-China.

About 15 in. *Cock:* A soft, rather greyish green with a bluish sheen on the nape and central tail feathers, more grey on the under parts and yellowish on the under wing coverts. The outer tail feathers are yellow on the inner webs and green on the outer and all are tipped with yellow. There is a black line from the nostrils to the eyes and a broad black line running downwards from the base of the beak and across the sides of the neck followed by a rose-red collar. Irides pale yellow; beak dark red; legs and feet yellowish-grey. *Hen:* Lacks the black lines on the head, and the rose-red collar, the latter being replaced by a rather indistinct

band of emerald green. Young birds also lack this marking and it may not develop until the birds are two years old.

Brought from India to Europe by the Romans, this was one of the first species of parrot to become a popular pet. These parrakeets will live amicably with other large birds, although some specimens are pugnacious and the pair must then be given accommodation to themselves.

Care must be taken during the mating time as the cock is then apt to become more fiery and bad-tempered although, in common with all of this group, it is more often the hen becomes aggressive and dominates her mate. A breeding pair is best kept quite separately.

If a roomy nest box is hung up in which some sawdust, wood shavings and crumbled pieces of rotten wood have been placed, the hen will begin to gnaw everything inside into shape ready to receive her eggs. This preparation will take her days to complete. Once everything is to her liking, she will reappear and the birds will begin to bill and coo all day long, while the cock whistles melodious flute-like notes. When the 3 – 4 eggs have been laid the hen once more takes to the nest and remains unseen until the young are hatched. These are then fed by both cock and hen with ripe sweet fruit, together with germinated oats, hemp, sunflower, canary seed and millet. Rusks soaked in milk and some fresh ants' eggs are also eaten.

These parrakeets can remain outside summer and winter, but should be confined to the shelter at night during hard weather as they are apt to lose their toes from frost-bite. Breeding begins in early spring, sometimes even before that. The first breeding results were recorded in Britain in 1902. A lutino and a blue variety were bred in India in 1932 and in 1941, and since 1951 these mutations have been repeatedly bred in Britain. An albino has also recently been produced.

Young birds taken from the nest and reared by hand become very tame and learn to talk well. They should not be kept near a cage or flight of other parrots or parrakeets if they are required as 'talkers'.

**Moustached Parrakeet** (Banded Parrakeet) *Psittacula alexandri fasciata*
*Origin* India and South China (Himalayas to Tonkin)

15 in. *Cock:* Head blue-grey. Line across the forehead and lores black, as well as a broad stripe running from the beak across base of cheeks. Throat band bright green. Back green, breast rosy lilac; remainder of under parts green. Wings green with a yellow-green shoulder spot. Eyes yellow. Upper mandible red, lower black. Legs grey-yellow. *Hen:* Shows little variation, but is a trifle bluer in colour and has a black beak.

This parrakeet is much more rarely found in private collections.

Treatment as for previous species. These birds should be kept only in pairs, as they are usually intolerant and very restless and are unsuitable to associate with others. A single specimen may well be kept by itself as a cage pet, for which purpose a young bird should be selected. It will soon grow tame and will learn to speak a few words. Moreover, a tame bird will not screech so unpleasantly. This screeching is an indication of fright and consequent distress, and is soon discontinued when confidence is restored. The Moustached Parrakeet is more suitable for a cage than the Indian Ring-necked Parrakeet, which is a little too active and noisy. The former is quiet in both habits and voice.

A pair may breed if housed by themselves and supplied with a large nest box and stimulating food. First records of breeding success came from the USA in 1929.

**Plum-headed Parrakeet** *Psittacula cyanocephala cyanocephala* Pl. 86
*Origin* India and Ceylon

14 in. *Cock:* Yellowish-green with a rose-purple head passing to violet-blue at back and with a narrow black collar edged with blue. Flights and long tail are shaded with yellow and pale blue, the end of the central tail feathers being almost white. There is a dark crimson bar on shoulder, and beak is yellow and black. *Hen:* Head is dark lavender-grey and shoulder bar is absent. Young birds are similar to the hen.

These parrakeets are beautifully coloured and not too large. Very tolerant towards other birds, they can be kept with foreign finches and other parrakeets, but for breeding purposes a pair should be given an aviary to themselves.

Their voice is not harsh or unpleasant, and when kept as a pair the calls of the cock are even quite melodious during the mating time.

Care is necessary with the acclimatization of newly-imported birds; they have to be accustomed to a seed diet. Much green food and willow twigs are necessary as well as sweet and ripe fruit. Oats, canary seed and hemp form the normal bill of fare, varied with some sunflower, ears of nearly ripe wheat, grass seeds and germinated grain.

A nest box of 8 in. by 12 in. hung in a light spot, so that the birds can perch on top of it, should be provided, and sawdust and wood shavings supplied to form a soft bed for the eggs. After the hen has arranged things to her liking, she will lay her 4–6 eggs and incubate them without assistance from the cock. Only when the young are 10 days old will she leave the nest. During the period of incubation and the early stages of rearing the cock has to cater for the whole family.

Germany reported breeding results for the first time in 1879, and Britain in 1898.

Soaked bread, hard-boiled egg, ants' eggs and mealworms must be made available during the rearing of the youngsters.

This is one of the most delightful of the parrot species and they make a brave show even in a smallish flight. There is a very similar bird from Indo-China and Burmah, the Blossom-headed Parrakeet, *Psittacula cyanocephala rosa* which is slightly smaller and has a paler head. Both cock and hen have the red shoulder bar.

**Malabar Parrakeet** *Psittacula columboides*
*Origin* Southern India

14½ in. *Cock:* Head, neck, breast and back grey, band across forehead green edged with blue, orbital ring and lores green. Around head and neck runs a black and blue band. Remainder of body entirely green, somewhat lighter yellowish-green on under parts. Flights green and blue, tail blue with a yellow tip. Eye brown, beak red, with under mandible blackish red. Legs grey-green. *Hen:* Lacks the neck band, and neck and breast are pale green instead of grey. Beak blackish.

These parrakeets are related to the Plum-headed Parrakeet, *Psittacula c. cyanocephala*, and need the same great care in acclimatization. In their natural state they feed almost exclusively on fruit and this is essential, in addition to the seed menu. Green food should certainly not be lacking, especially in the early stages of acclimatization. Fresh willow twigs must be available. Oats, sunflower, canary seed and hemp should be given daily. The birds will learn to eat apples and soaked bread, particularly during the rearing season. They will also take mealworms at that time. Once they have become used to apples, they will prefer that fruit to any other.

Successful breeding depends mainly on correct feeding. If there is insufficient variety, or if fruit and green food are left out of the diet, failure is inevitable.

These birds are sometimes considered dull and uninteresting because they hide in the branches during the daytime and only come down to eat and drink. However, they can be kept together with other and larger parrakeets and this is an advantage. They will snap at smaller birds that dare to approach their perches, but a fight never takes place. They can winter outside and are among the hardiest of aviary birds. The first breeding results were reported in Britain in 1926.

**Barraband Parrakeet** *Polytelis swainsonii* Pl. 88
*Origin* East and south-east Australia

*Cock:* Brilliant grass-green; forehead, throat and cheeks yellow with an orange-red crescent on throat. Wings greenish-blue. Tail green-blue. Eye orange-yellow. Beak orange-red, legs brown, sometimes with red thighs.

*Hen:* Pale green, lacking the yellow on head and crescent.

Breeding results have been reported repeatedly. Like the Rosella, these parrakeets commence nesting very early in spring and should be provided with a deep nest box or hollow log hung in the outside aviary.

Diet consists of the normal mixture for large parrakeets; canary seed and hemp are especially important.

They are hardy and can stay in the outside aviary summer and winter. Breeding results first reported in France in 1881 and in Britain in 1900. Crossings with the Rock Peplar have been reported and have proved fertile.

**Rock Peplar Parrakeet** (Rock Pebbler Parrakeet, Black-tailed Parrakeet) *Polytelis anthopeplus* Pl. 91
*Origin* South and West Australia

15¼ in. *Cock:* Pale yellow with a greenish tone; rump, secondaries and whole of under parts yellow. Wings black with yellow and red on shoulders. Tail black with a bluish sheen. Eye and beak red, legs black. *Hen:* More olive-brown than yellow, and has brown tail coverts, tail feathers being edged with salmon pink. Sexing is facilitated by this difference in the colouring of the tail.

In addition to the seed menu of canary seed, hemp sunflower seed and ground nuts, fruit should be provided regularly, particularly apples, fresh leaf buds and, now and again, some honey.

These very hardy birds can winter outside, always providing that a well-covered shelter is available. They will also breed well in the outdoor aviary, if the flight is roomy and quiet. They need an enclosure at least 25 ft long by 7 ft wide, and if at all possible 7 to 10 ft high.

Some rotten wood should be placed in the bottom of a deep nest-box and this will be chewed up by the birds and will form a moist bed on which the eggs will be deposited.

During breeding, the proportion of hemp seed can be increased and meal-worms may be supplied although some birds refuse to eat them. They bred for the first time in Britain as long ago as 1865. Various crossings with related species have proved successful.

**Princess of Wales Parrakeet** (Queen Alexandra's Parrakeet) *Polytelis alexandrae* Pl. 89
*Origin* Central and north-western Australia

17 in. *Cock:* Forehead, crown and nape light blue; hind neck, upper back, scapulars and inner secondaries olive-green; lower back and rump blue; upper tail coverts light olive-green, two central tail feathers olive-green fading into bluish-green at the tips and edged with greenish-yellow at base, next on either side similar but with the basel half of the inner webs pink, remainder pale bluish-grey broadly edged with rose-pink and tipped with greenish-yellow. Upper wing coverts yellowish-green, primary coverts indigo-blue, innermost secondaries pale olive-green, remainder green on the outer webs, tinged with blue at the tips and greenish-white on the outer edges, outer flights also tinged with blue. Lores and below the eyes yellowish-green; chin, cheeks and throat rose-pink; remainder of under surface pale olive-green with a wash of grey-blue on the abdomen; thighs dull rose-red; sides of flanks deep blue and lilac. Irides bright orange; red

orbital ring, beak coral-red, whitish at tip; legs and feet dark grey. *Hen:* Similar but slightly smaller and much paler in colouring, the primary coverts washed with green. Lacks the red orbital ring.

This, again, is one of the more costly birds, which is, however, found in many private collections, and is fairly extensively bred in the United Kingdom.

It needs the same treatment as does the Crimson-winged Parrakeet.

These birds are at their most graceful in a large and roomy aviary, where they will usually settle down to breed. The mating time is interesting and their love-making is captivating to watch. They seem to embrace, and sit cheek to cheek. After long preliminaries mating takes place and two days later laying commences. After the third or fourth egg is laid, the hen begins to incubate. The cock feeds her during the 20 days she is sitting.

The food should consist of millet, canary seed, sunflower, oats, and soaked bread and they are very fond of hemp – but this should be given sparingly. A quantity of green food, chickweed and especially lettuce, also fruit such as apples and pears are needed. Their young should also be reared on this diet.

The nest box or log nest must be large – at least 24 inches deep. A quantity of willow or poplar chips must be placed on the bottom together with sawdust. The former help to supply humidity.

The young birds leave the nest after 5 weeks and then resemble the parent birds, except that their colouring is much duller. It seems to be certain that they are sufficiently developed to breed when a year old.

Unfortunately, it is difficult to obtain birds of good stamina. There were only a few pairs imported originally and in-breeding has caused many birds to become sterile. The use of an imported cock is therefore advisable if such a bird can be obtained.

Although they need ample space for their special morning and evening activities, they can be kept together with all kinds of other birds such as parrakeets and foreign finches with complete safety. The one exception is their own kind.

They are hardy and may winter in an outside flight. They were bred for the first time in 1899 and in Britain in 1912.

A blue mutation appeared in Australia in 1951. Crossing with the Barraband and the Rock Peplar has been reported, also with the Indian Ring-necked Parrakeet and the Crimson-winged Parrakeet.

**Crimson-winged Parrakeet** *Aprosmictus erythropterus erythropterus* Pl. 90

*Origin* North-western and northern Australia, Queensland and New South Wales

12 in. *Cock:* Forehead and sides of head light green; crown, nape and hind neck bluish-green; back and shoulders black; lower back and rump ultra-marine blue; upper tail coverts yellowish-green; outer wing coverts rich crimson; secondaries and flights blackish, edged with dark green on the outer webs; tail dark green tipped with pale yellowish-green; under parts entirely rich green; irides red; beak orange-red; legs and feet brown. *Hen:* General colour green, less intense than cock; lacks the black on back and shoulders and the crimson area of the wings replaced with red, most of the

feathers being edged with dull green; lateral tail feathers edged with pink on inner webs; under surface pale yellowish-green; beak dull orange.

Only a few fanciers are fortunate enough to possess this species and, unfortunately, it cannot be described as free breeding. They are not readily obtainable and are always expensive.

Like others of their genus, they are best kept as a pair in a flight to themselves, and under these conditions may be persuaded to nest. The nest box should be at least 12 in. by 16 in., and not less than 36 in. deep, and should be placed in a light position in the open flight.

In addition to millet, oats, hemp and canary seed, soaked maize or corn on the cob should be given. Fruit, apples and various stone fruit and berries are also needed. Plenty of green food and fresh twigs of beech, birch, lime and willow trees should be provided.

Variety is important, and during the breeding season germinated seed must be given. It will soon be evident which kind is preferred. Rusks or stale soaked bread with hard-boiled egg and some ants' eggs for the rearing of the young are readily accepted.

These birds like to be on the move; they clamber and fly, and therefore need a largish flight. They soon get bored in a cage, and will just sit and mope all day. Outside of the breeding time they can quite well be kept with other birds. The cock will, however, chase away every intruder from the vicinity of the nest, and some cocks become exceedingly rough with their own hens during the breeding season, even killing them if they do not go to nest. Should a cock develop these savage tendencies, it is as well to clip the flight feathers of one wing. This will handicap him sufficiently to enable the hen to keep beyond his reach.

Breeding results were obtained in Germany in 1878 and in France in 1881.

The hen will usually incubate without assistance from the cock. After the eggs have been hatched, it will be a month or so before the young appear. Once they become independent they should be separated from their parents.

Crossing with the King Parrakeet and also with the Queen Alexandra Parrakeet has been reported.

**Green-winged King Parrakeet** *Alisterus chloropterus chloropterus* Pl. 93
*Origin* South-east New Guinea

15½ in. *Cock:* Very similar to the King Parrakeet, *A. scapularis*, but the light green band across the shoulders is much wider and the blue areas on the nape and rump more extensive. *Hen:* also similar to hen King Parrakeet.

Feeding and treatment should be as for the King Parrakeet which this species closely resembles in all respects.

**King Parrakeet** *Alisterus scapularis scapularis* Pl. 94
*Origin* South Australia

15¼ in. *Cock:* Head and under parts scarlet, nape band and rump blue, back green, wings green with blue and a light green band across shoulders. Tail black with olive-green edges. Secondaries dark olive-green, under tail coverts blue edged with scarlet. Beak red, legs grey. *Hen:* Head and upper parts green, throat, neck and upper part of breast green with a dull red shading. Rump blue, belly scarlet under tail coverts green, neck and breast olive-green with a pinkish gloss. Tail green and black, beak grey.

They are expensive but can be recommended for breeding purposes,

Only in a very roomy flight, with a quiet situation where a pair can be kept alone, is there a chance that breeding will be successful. Quite frequently the hen will refuse to use a nest box and will lay her eggs in a scrape made in the floor of the flight or shelter. There she will successfully incubate and rear her young, but these conditions are far from ideal. A deep and roomy nest box either hung up or set on the floor should be provided, with a good layer of rotten wood chips in the bottom. Its size should be 14 in. by 14 in. and 34 to 44 in. deep. The layer of wood pulp should be quite 6 in. deep. The best position is always in the open air.

In Australia these birds are most destructive to the maize crops. This grain should certainly be included in their diet, together with canary seed, hemp, ground nuts and sunflower seed. Fruit, especially apples, and green food must be supplied daily.

The cocks are very ferocious during the nesting period. The youngsters do not attain their full colouring until the third year. These parrakeets bred for the first time in Britain in 1876. They are quite unsuitable for cage life indoors as they will not survive in such a warm temperature. They are very hardy and can winter out of doors. Hybrids have been produced with the Crimson-winged Parrakeet and the Barraband Parrakeet.

**Madagascar Lovebird** (Grey-headed Lovebird) *Agapornis cana cana* Pl. 95

*Origin* Madagascar

5–6 in. *Cock:* Mostly green, lighter on the belly, darker on the wings. The head, neck and upper part of breast are grey. Tail green and black. Beak pale

horn coloured; feet pale grey. *Hen:* Can easily be distinguished as she lacks the grey colouring of the head and breast.

On the whole, these are quiet birds although the hen becomes aggressive and eager to fight during the breeding season, and at that time may be dangerous to other birds.

In any case it is advisable to accommodate breeding pairs on their own. They will nest in a hollow log and the nest is constructed from twigs, bark and straw. The hen inserts the nesting materials in the feathers around the rump and thus decorated enters the nest. She loses several bits and pieces on the way but in spite of that she will build a bulky nest and even when eggs have been laid, will continue to enlarge it. It is, therefore, advisable to supply a roomy nest box.

The Madagascar is shy at first but soon becomes accustomed to its new surroundings and settles down.

For a time this species completely disappeared from the market but it is now obtainable again in limited numbers.

It is recorded that a Madagascar did once learn to say a few words. This bird had been bred at home, was finger tame, and had been kept out of sight and sound of its own kind.

This and all the other species of *Agapornis* require the same treatment and food. Diet should consist of canary seed, millet, sunflower and some hemp. During the breeding season the hemp may be increased. Soaked stale brown bread, lots of apple and green food should also figure on the daily menu.

Fresh willow twigs are necessary for nest building and to provide the birds with a suitable material to gnaw, as this is most beneficial to their general health.

The first breeding results were reported in Britain in 1882, and in Germany earlier still, in 1872, by Russ. It is claimed that the species has hybridized with a Budgerigar.

**Red-faced Lovebird** *Agapornis pullaria pullaria*
*Origin* East and West Africa.

6 in. *Cock:* Bright green, more yellowish on the under parts; face and crown orange-red; rump bright blue; bend of wing, shoulder and under wing coverts black, edge of wing bluish, flights dusky with green outer webs; tail green with a band of red followed by a band of black towards the tip; irides brown; beak red; legs and feet dark grey. *Hen:* Red of the face less bright and more orange in tone; rump paler blue; under wing coverts green; edge of wing yellowish.

Although regularly imported in the past and easily kept, these birds will seldom produce young. The German and French names 'inseparables' suggest that these birds will only live if kept together in pairs, but in fact a single bird can be kept by itself for years on end. But if and when a pair has been obtained and a warm spot has been selected for cage or flight, their vivid colouring and lively behaviour, will ensure their popularity. These Lovebirds may safely be kept together with other birds of medium size in a roomy flight.

Acclimatization after importation is apt to give trouble, and care must be taken with the birds. Those which seem unhealthy on arrival are usually difficult to establish. But once they become used to climate and food, they will survive and give little trouble.

Green stuff should be given regularly, especially if young are being fed; stale bread soaked in water, egg yolk and some fresh or dried ants' eggs are also indispensable. When wild these birds breed not in a hollow tree but in the ant hills constructed by termites. Hence in captivity artificial ant hills of loam must be provided with suitable tunnels to serve as nesting cavities. These are rather difficult to make, and few breeding results have been recorded. Bales of compressed peat have been successfully used as a substitute for the loam.

There is ample opportunity for any fancier to specialize in this species.

**Peach-faced Lovebird** (Rosy-faced Lovebird) *Agapornis roseicollis* Pl. 96
*Origin* Southern Angola, south to the Orange River.

6 in. *Cock:* Bright almond-green, more yellow on under side; forehead deep rose-red, side of head and throat pale rose; rump and upper tail coverts bright blue; flights blackish, under wing coverts bluish-green; tail green, the outer feathers orange-red at base and with a black, subterminal bar. Irides brown; beak whitish-horn, legs and feet grey. *Hen:* Similar and difficult to distinguish, face sometimes paler in colour.

Regularly obtainable as they are freely bred in captivity.

A characteristic feature is the curious fashion in which the hen carries the bits of bark to the nest-box. She places them between the feathers on her back and, when she is rigged out with many bits and looks really ridiculous, she clambers carefully to the nest box, holding her feathers rigid, but still losing some of her load on the way.

The birds themselves keep their nest

damp by constantly adding fresh green bark and by carrying in water, on their feathers, so that the boxes need not be hung where the rain can get at them. They are sufficiently hardy to stay out during the winter. One pair only should be put in an aviary when breeding, as they are fierce fighters among themselves. They should be treated like the other species of Lovebirds.

First breeding results were reported from Germany in 1860 and from Britain in 1895.

Budgerigars have successfully been used to hatch and rear young Peachfaced Lovebirds.

A yellow variety was obtained in the USA in 1929. Hybrids have been produced with the Masked, the Nyassa and the Black-cheeked Lovebirds. It is also claimed to have been crossed with the Budgerigar.

**Abyssinian Lovebird** (Black-winged Lovebird) *Agapornis taranta taranta* Pl. 97
*Origin* Abyssinia.

6½ in. *Cock:* Forehead and orbital ring red. Upper parts green, rump and upper tail coverts lighter green, under parts also lighter green. Wing coverts and primaries brown-black. Tail feathers green with a wide black cross band towards the tips. Beak dark red, eye brown, legs grey. *Hen:* Like the cock, but lacks the red on the head. As it is quite simple to select a true pair and since the care and upkeep presents no difficulties, these Lovebirds should enjoy a greater popularity with fanciers.

At first they are very shy and timid but they soon become accustomed to their new surroundings and lose their timidity. They make less noise than some other species so are suitable for keeping together in pairs, in the house.

In addition to a seed mixture of millet, canary seed and oats, they like apple, and pear and the bark of willow twigs to chew. They use willow bark for their nest building. The nest is constructed in a large hollow log and 2–4 youngsters are reared. Soaked stale brown bread, as well as germinated seed, forms the staple ingredients of the rearing diet.

When the young first emerge from the nest, their beaks are dull yellow.

A pair may safely be kept together with larger parrakeets or other birds which are able to defend themselves against possible intimidation, but housing them with others of their own kind invariably results in frequent fights, often with fatal consequences, for the beaks of these birds can cause severe injuries. If it is desired to keep several pairs together, it is essential to hang up a larger number of nest boxes than the number of pairs of birds on hand, for most quarrels arise over the possession of a nest box.

The first breeding results were obtained in Germany in 1925 and in Britain in 1926.

Slower in commencing to breed than other Lovebirds, the Abyssinian are able to withstand cold better and there is little risk in leaving them out-of-doors during the winter months, always providing that a dry shelter is available.

They are said to have hybridized with Fischer's and Masked Lovebirds.

**Fischer's Lovebird** *Agapornis personata fischeri*
*Origin* North-west Tanganyika Territory Pl. 98

5½ in. *Cock* and *Hen* alike. Green, paler and more yellowish on under parts; forehead bright orange-red, crown dusky olive, nape orange; cheeks and throat paler orange slightly washed with olive; rump and upper tail coverts bright blue; flights blackish with green on the outer webs; tail green, central feathers tipped with pale blue, outer feathers orange at base with a subterminal band of black and blue tips; irides brown; beak coral-red; legs and feet dark grey. There is a white naked orbital ring.

The first breeding results were obtained by the Duke of Bedford in 1927.

Like the Masked, this species is at present regularly available as many are bred annually. Hybrids with the Masked, the Nyassa, the Black-cheeked and the Peach-faced have been reported.

They will breed as readily as the Masked Lovebird. Crossing with the Blue Masked has succeeded so that in time a blue Fischer's may be expected, providing of course that the hybrid Fischer's × Blue Masked prove to be fertile.

The Masked and Fischer's are species which may easily be kept by a beginner and give much pleasure. The birds are hardy and can remain outside during the winter. They are no more noisy or disturbing than ordinary budgerigars, though perhaps too noisy to be kept in a living-room.

A humid atmosphere is essential to them. Nest boxes should therefore be hung up outside, where the rain can get at them. The treatment is otherwise exactly the same as for other species of Lovebirds.

**Masked Lovebird** *Agapornis personata personata*
*Origin* North-eastern Tanganyika Territory Pl. 99

5¾ in. Sexes alike. Head, including ear coverts and cheeks dull brownish-black; a yellow collar round the nape of the neck, extending to the breast where it merges into the green of the body colour; rump and upper tail coverts washed with grey-blue; flights black with green outer webs; tail green, outer feathers orange at base and with black bar and yellowish tips. Irides brown; beak red; legs and feet dark grey. Naked orbital ring white.

These birds are most suitable for breeding either in a cage or in the aviary or flight, where several pairs can be kept together. In a breeding cage there should be only one pair.

Fresh willow twigs are indispensable; the birds will fill up the nest boxes with bark stripped from these twigs and make a tunnel entrance and nesting cavity in the centre.

A damp atmosphere is harmful to them. They breed best in spring and autumn. In summer they have a natural period of rest which coincides with the driest months of the year. In winter the birds take no notice of the cold and will go on breeding if allowed, but winter is not the best time for this.

Nest boxes with two floors are recommended as the hen will often start laying the second clutch while the young are still in the first nest. The old birds also like roosting in the nest box and then use the 'first floor'.

A handsome colour mutation has been bred from which the yellow pigment has been eliminated. As a result the green has become blue and the yellow has become white. This variety is now known as the Blue Masked Lovebird and was first bred in Britain in 1930. Japan produced a white variety in 1940 and a lutino variety was bred in the USA in 1935.

The young can be successfully reared on soaked stale brown bread with a few drops of cod liver oil. I myself reared two birds born in the month of January on baby rusks soaked in milk or orange juice, with some cod liver oil added. I fed them with an ear syringe and they soon became so used to this that they immediately opened their mouths wide whenever the syringe appeared. With this treatment they rapidly became tame and thrived well. They soon started eating seed on their own and when fully developed were equal to any other of their species.

Hybrids of the Masked Lovebird and the Peach-faced Lovebird have been produced, and also between the Masked and the Black-cheeked Lovebird.

## Nyassa Lovebird *Agapornis personata lilianae*

*Origin* Northern Rhodesia to Nyasaland and south to the Zambesi.

4¾ in. Sexes alike. Dark green on the back and wings, lighter green below, yellowish on rump and upper tail coverts; head, throat and upper breast salmon-pink, brighter on forehead and pale on cheeks; nape yellowish-green; flights dusky green; tail green, outer feathers with orange at base and with a black bar and green tips. Irides yellow to reddish-brown; beak red; legs and feet grey; naked orbital ring white.

These are one of the smallest of the Lovebirds; they are usually obtainable and a lutino variety, which was first produced in Australia, can now be bought, although only hens of this mutation appear to be available so far. The species was first bred in Britain in 1926.

The charm of this species is that the birds breed so well in a colony. They will build their nest of twigs, straw, bark and empty millet sprays in the nest boxes provided, and they go on breeding practically all the year round. Incubation takes 3 weeks. It is not advisable to keep them outside during the winter since they will persist in roosting in the nest boxes in the open flight and will continue to produce eggs and hatch young until the hens become completely exhausted and the young die. It is therefore better from every point of view to take these birds into a heated room in winter and no nest boxes should be supplied until they are returned to the open aviary in the following spring.

Like the other Lovebirds they live on canary seed, millet, sunflower seed, hemp, millet in the spray, and quantities of apples and green food. They should be given soaked bread during the breeding season.

They have a bad habit of plucking the young whilst they are in the nest. This habit seems congenital to this species, although it has been checked to some extent by adding cod liver oil and lime to the seed ration. The cause is still a mystery but is probably due to a diet deficiency.

This species has been successfully crossed with the Black-cheeked, Peach-faced, and Fischer's Lovebirds, the use of either cock or hen giving equally satisfactory results.

## Black-cheeked Lovebird *Agapornis personata nigrigenis*

*Origin* Northern Rhodesia

5½ in. Resembles the Nyassa Lovebird, but the mask is brown instead of orange and the ear coverts almost black. It also has a salmon-coloured spot on the breast, a red beak and the white orbital ring which is common to all the closely related subspecies of *Agapornis personata*.

*Cock* and *Hen* are difficult to tell apart. The eyes of the hen are said to be of a lighter brown than those of the cock.

The crossing of the Black-cheeked Lovebird and the Nyassa Lovebird produces a fertile intermediary form. If there were a doubt whether the Nyassa Lovebirds belong to the *personata* group, the production of these fertile hybrids has supplied convincing proof of their close relationship.

Owing to the ease with which these crosses can be effected and the great number of hybrids which have been produced and distributed, it is becoming increasingly difficult to obtain stock which can be guaranteed to be pure bred. In fact the only certain way is to purchase birds which have been freshly imported from their native land. The Black-cheeked Lovebird has the reputation of being a free breeder, and is also very tolerant in a colony. The first breeding results were obtained in the United Kingdom in 1908.

Care and treatment should be given as for the other Lovebirds. Crossings have been successful with the Peach-faced, Masked, Fischer's and Nyassa Lovebird and, it is claimed, with the Budgerigar.

**Blue-crowned Hanging Parrot** *Loriculus galgulus galgulus* Pl. 100

*Origin* Wellesley Province to Singapore, Sumatra, Nias, Bangka and Borneo.

Not quite 5 in. *Cock:* Green with a dark blue spot on crown, a triangular golden spot on upper back, a bright yellow band across lower back, rump and upper tail coverts scarlet; tail green with yellowish tip; large scarlet bib; under wing and under tail bluish-green; irides brown; cere and beak black; legs and feet greyish-brown. *Hen:* Much duller, with no scarlet on throat nor yellow band on lower back.

These are most charming little birds to keep as a pair in a room aviary or cage. Unfortunately, they are not often obtainable.

The keeping of these birds with others in an aviary is not recommended; their excreta is copious, thin in consistency, and occurs so frequently that other birds and nests soon become soiled.

During sleep these birds hang upside down from a branch or perch and this is an indication that they are in good health, for sick birds never suspend themselves in this way. Their voices are soft and rather pleasing.

They breed in parrakeet nesting boxes, into which they will bring small bits of bark chewed from willow twigs. They bred in Germany in 1907.

Their diet should consist of rice boiled in water, grated apple, various seeds, groats and millet in the spray. Now and again baby rusks soaked in orange juice or other fruit juice, and honey made liquid with boiling water and given in solution when cold should be provided. Hard-boiled egg or raw egg yolk mixed with toasted breadcrumbs and ants' eggs help to make up a varied diet. The seed supply should be limited at first but can be gradually increased. Fruit and fruit juice must always be given, but the food should not be made too moist. The birds can take more moisture if they wish and it is best to let them determine the quantity themselves.

They are very active, and like to clamber about the branches in the aviary.

The next two species require the same treatment:

**Ceylon Hanging Parrot** *Loriculus beryllinus*
*Origin* Ceylon

5½ in. *Cock:* Green, paler below; crown, rump and upper tail coverts red; nape and mantle washed with orange; lores, cheeks, chin and throat bluish; irides white, cere yellow; beak orange-red; legs and feet dull yellow. *Hen:* Similar but smaller with broader and more rounded beak.

**Vernal Hanging Parrot** *Loriculus vernalis vernalis*
*Origin* India, through the Indo-Burmese countries and Malay Peninsula

6¾ in. *Cock:* Green with orange wash on upper back; rump and upper tail coverts red; flights bluish on inner webs; throat with bluish patch; yellowish wash on upper breast; irides yellowish-white, eyelids yellowish, cere red; beak dull red, legs and feet pale orange with pinkish claws. *Hen:* More yellowish green with dull green head and the blue of the throat very faint or entirely absent.

**Pennant's Parrakeet** (Crimson Rosella) *Platycercus elegans elegans* Pl. 101
*Origin* Eastern and South Australia and Kangaroo Island

15 in. *Cock:* General colour deep crimson; cheeks violet-blue; back black, the feathers edged with crimson; flights black with blue on the outer webs; median secondaries edged with light blue; innermost edged with dull crimson upper wing coverts blue; tail, central feathers dark blue washed with green, outer feathers pale blue with whitish tips. Irides dark brown;

beak horn; legs and feet blackish. *Hen:* Similar but with noticeably smaller head and sometimes the crimson of the upper parts is less vivid and the tail more greenish. Immature birds of both sexes are greenish with red lacing to the feathers, only the forehead being red.

These birds can be bought fairly regularly, but they are always expensive. When buying, the proviso should also be made that an exchange be permitted if both birds should prove to be of the same sex.

A pair can be kept in an outside aviary together with small birds, but not with other parrakeets. Crimson Rosellas are gorgeously coloured, and are always on the move, clambering on branches or amusing themselves busily on the floor. Their voice is usually heard in the evening and they will whistle melodiously.

They are also fairly reliable breeders, but a careful watch should be kept on the cock as at that time he is apt to become savage and to persecute his hen unless she readily accepts his advances. They have not, unfortunately, proved to be as prolific as the Common and Mealy Rosellas.

The usual type of nest box and the correct rearing food must, of course, be provided as with the Common Rosella.

They can winter outside, if a well-covered shelter is available. They were first bred in Britain in 1880. Many crossings with other species – Mealy, Brown's, Adelaide and Yellow-rumped Parrakeets – have been recorded.

**Adelaide Parrakeet** *Platycercus adelaidae* Pl. 104
*Origin* South and Central Australia

15 in. *Cock:* Differs from Pennant's

Parrakeet in being brick red, this colour being mixed with yellow. The feathers of the back and the upper parts are black edged with buff and yellow and the tail is more green, only slightly washed with blue. The blue of the cheeks is much paler. *Hen:* Differs from the cock just as the hen of Pennant's Parrakeet differs from the cock of that species.

Outwardly this Rosella shows a great resemblance to the Pennant's and it has been said, but not proved, that it originated from a natural cross between Pennant's and the Yellow-rumped Parrakeet. Such hybrids have been produced already in Britain, and it has been shown that the fertile offspring will continue to produce birds which exactly resemble Adelaides. The Adelaide was first bred in the United Kingdom in 1907.

Treatment as for other Rosellas described.

## Yellow Rosella (Yellow-rumped Parrakeet) *Platycerus flaveolus* Pl. 107

*Origin* Interior of New South Wales and adjoining parts of Victoria and South Australia

12 in. *Cock:* General colour above and below pale yellow; feathers of back and scapulars with black centres; forehead with a narrow band of crimson immediately above the beak and the lores and fore-neck slightly tinged with the same colour; cheeks blue; wings, flights blackish with blue on the outer webs, outer secondaries edged with pale blue, inner ones and also inner wing coverts edged with pale yellow, outer wing coverts pale blue and lesser coverts dark blue with a black patch; tail, two central feathers blue with greenish tone at base, next pair blackish

with blue on the outer webs and tipped with blue, remainder blue, paler towards the tips; irides black; beak horn coloured; legs and feet greyish-black. *Hen:* Similar but with smaller head and beak. Immature birds of both sexes are dull greenish-yellows with the other colours and the dark markings much paler and the latter sometimes almost absent.

This species is hardy and is said to be a free breeder in captivity. Its treatment and feeding should be as described for other Rosellas.

It was first bred in England in 1892 and is said to have crossed with the Common Rosella.

## Common Rosella (Eastern Rosella, Red Rosella) *Platycercus eximius eximius*

*Origin* South-eastern Australia

13 in. *Cock:* Head, sides of neck and upper breast scarlet cheeks white; nape yellow, back and scapulars black, the feathers being edged with greenish-yellow; rump and upper tail coverts yellowish-green; flights blackish, dark blue on the outer webs; secondaries edged with light blue, primary coverts dark blue, lesser, median and outer series violet-blue with a black patch on the inner series; tail feathers dark blue, those in centre washed with green and the outer tipped with whitish-blue; lower breast yellow; abdomen yellowish-green; under tail coverts scarlet. Irides dark brown; beak bluish-horn; legs and feet dark grey. *Hen:* Similar but duller in general colouring.

Aviary-bred birds of this colourful species are usually on offer. They can be kept together with small birds, which they will leave in peace, but with other parrakeets they become rather aggressive.

Although they are not more difficult to keep than the Barnard's Parrakeet, they are less dependable breeders. The call of the cock is a rather pleasing whistle. The hen's call note is shorter and less musical.

Their principal food is oats, especially when germinated, canary seed and millet, and also millet sprays. Sunflower and hemp in limited quantities, as well as half-ripened wheat ears, can be recommended. Fruit of every kind and green stuff are indispensable. Fresh twigs from various trees should not be omitted.

These parrakeets usually start nesting in early spring. The hen alone will incubate the 4–6 eggs. When the young leave the nest, they are usually extremely nervous and are apt to fly hard against the wire netting. They soon become accustomed to the limitations of their aviary however, and within a couple of days this nervous phase will pass. They were first bred in Spain in 1862. Hybrids have been produced with the Pennant's, Adelaide, Stanley and Brown's Parrakeets, Mealy Rosella and the Cockatiel.

Rearing food should consist of seed and soaked bread with hard-boiled eggs and ants' eggs, together with raw carrot and green stuff.

These parrakeets are hardy and can safely be wintered outside.

**Golden-mantled Rosella** (Yellow-mantled Rosella) *Platycercus eximius cecilae* Pl. 105

*Origin* Southern Queensland and interior of New South Wales.

*Cock:* As large as the Common Rosella, but on the whole deeper in colouring. The ground colour of the black laced feathers of the back is golden yellow instead of pale green and the abdomen is also golden with a reddish tinge. The under tail coverts are blue-green. *Hen:* Similar but the colours less brilliant.

Although extensively bred in Great Britain, it has too frequently been crossed with the Common Rosella and the stock has deteriorated. It is now difficult to obtain really pure bred birds. The first breeding was reported in the United Kingdom in 1934.

Treatment should be exactly the same as that for the other Rosellas.

**Stanley Parrakeet** (Western Rosella) *Platycercus icterotis icterotis* Pl. 102

*Origin* South-western Australia

11 in. *Cock:* Crown, nape, breast and under parts crimson; cheeks and thighs yellow; back black, each feather laced with green, yellow and sometimes with crimson; rump and upper tail coverts golden-green; shoulders blue; flights blackish with the outer webs blue; tail, central pair of feathers dull green, the remainder pale blue tipped with white; irides dark brown, beak horn coloured; legs and feet dull grey-brown. *Hen:* Generally duller in colour with no red margins to the feathers of the back except in very old birds. Also smaller than cock and the red of the under parts sometimes finely margined with green.

Young cocks are usually duller in colour and the hens are a trifle smaller.

These are costly birds, though usually available as they are freely bred in captivity. They are one of the smallest of the Rosellas; brilliant in colouring.

A pair should be kept separately and given a choice of several nest boxes hung up in the open flight. Once they have chosen a nest, the remaining boxes should be removed. Two to three in. of sawdust or peat litter must be placed in the nest box. The 4 – 6 eggs are incubated solely by the hen. Once the young have hatched (which is evident by the sudden increased consumption of the rearing food), soaked rusks and egg, ants' eggs and germinated seeds must be provided. Green food and a fruit diet should not be overlooked. It is just as well not to interfere with the birds or the nest as privacy and quietness are essential at this time. Once the young have left the nest, the rearing food can be progressively reduced until it is discontinued entirely.

Normal diet should consist of millet, canary seed, sunflower and hemp. Sometimes the birds like groundnuts. Young green stuff, especially fresh shoots and germinated seed, can be given as a treat. The birds are not, however, fastidious; chickweed as green food, and apples as fruit, will suffice.

To induce them to breed, pairs should be housed separately. It is then quite possible that they will multiply sixfold in a season, since they are double brooded. The young can be kept safely with other small birds or with others of their own kind.

They are hardy birds and can winter in an unheated aviary.

**Mealy Rosella** (Pale-headed Rosella)
*Platycercus adscitus palliceps* Pl. 106
*Origin* Queensland and New South Wales

13 in. *Cock:* Head pale yellow, deeper towards the base of the nape; hind neck and scapulars and upper back black, each feather edged with rich yellow; lower back rump and upper tail coverts pale greenish-blue; upper wing coverts blue, darker on the shoulder; secondaries and flights dark blue, some of the former edged with dark blue and the latter with grey-white; tail, central pair of feathers dark blue with greenish wash at base, next pair blackish with dark blue on the outer webs and tipped with white, remainder pale blue shading to darker blue at the base and tipped with white; cheeks white with blue wash on outer border; under tail coverts scarlet; remainder of under parts pale blue; irides yellowish-brown, beak bluish-white; legs and feet dark grey. *Hen:* Slightly smaller with smaller head and beak; paler in colour. Immature birds of both sexes are much duller, with the entire plumage tinged with green.

Treatment does not differ from that described for other Roselles.

When it is desired to breed, the pair should be given an aviary to themselves as early as possible in the year. The first eggs will often be laid in February.

These birds are absolutely hardy, and their young are usually very tame. It is difficult to tell the cock from the hen, and an arrangement must be made at the time of purchase that an exchange can be effected later on, if necessary. If a proved breeding pair is offered for sale, this risk, of course, is not present, but an appreciably higher price may have to be paid.

The nest boxes should be provided with a layer of sawdust, which will usually be gratefully accepted. This also applies to all the other Rosellas.

These birds were first bred in Belgium in 1899. Crossings with the Pennant's and Stanley have been reported.

**Brown's Parrakeet** (Northern Rosella)
*Platycerus venustus venustus* Pl. 92
*Origin* North Australia

11½ in. *Cock:* Head and throat black. Plumage of back black with a dull yellow edge to the feathers. Remainder of upper surface pale yellow. Cheek patches white with a blue edge. Wings blue and black. Tail light and dark blue with white tips. Under tail coverts red. Beak horn-coloured, eyes and legs black. *Hen:* Colouring is slightly less intense and she is usually less bold in head.

This Rosella is costly and scarce. Cock and hen are very difficult to tell apart and it has happened repeatedly that attempts had been made to get two cocks or two hens to breed. Since the only stock at present available is homebred, the proviso should be made when purchasing that there should be an exchange if the two birds should not turn out to be a pair.

It is difficult to get the birds accustomed to breeding during the summer months as the moult starts about that time. If, however, they are allowed to breed during the winter, egg binding will often occur.

Should a true pair be obtained, and the birds put together in a well-sheltered outside aviary in January, with roomy nest boxes in different places, the hen will soon show her preference for a certain box. To prevent her laying a few eggs in one nest box and later moving to another, it is advisable to remove all boxes except the one first chosen.

First breeding results were reported in Britain in 1928. The species has also been crossed with both the Common and the Mealy Rosella.

These birds should be treated exactly like the other Rosellas. If they will not take ants' eggs and egg food for the rearing of the young, they should be offered mealworms, which are sometimes consumed avidly. Plenty of green food and fresh twigs are a necessity.

**Barnard's Parrakeet** (Mallee Parrakeet)
*Barnardius b. barnardi* Pl. 112
*Origin* Southern Queensland, New South Wales, Victoria and South Australia

14 in. *Cock:* Forehead red; crown, ear coverts and cheeks verditer-green, the latter edges with blue; nape with a dull bluish-brown band and a yellow band round the hind neck, broader at the sides; back and scapulars dull greyish-blue and a yellowish-green band down the centre of the upper wing coverts; rump and upper tail coverts verditer-green washed with yellow. Wing coverts and outer webs of flights deep blue, remainder green; tail, central pair of feathers green, blue towards the tips, remainder dark blue at base fading to pale blue towards the tips, under parts verditer-green with a broad band of orange-yellow across the breast; irides blackish-brown; beak, upper mandible pale horn, lower mandible bluish; legs and feet greyish-black. *Hen:* Differs in its duller colour and smaller size.

This species will live peaceably in the aviary and may be kept with other birds such as Cockatiels and Bourke's Parrakeets. Only when the mating time arrives are skirmishes apt to occur. The treatment should be as given to the Stanley Parrakeet. It is hardy and can winter out-of-doors.

Breeding results have been reported regularly in France from 1884 and in the United Kingdom for the first time in 1902.

They have been crossed with the Mealy Rosella, Common Rosella, Pennant's and Red-rumped Parrakeets.

### Red-rumped Parrakeet (Red-backed Parrakeet) *Psephotus h. haematonotus* Pl. 108, 111

*Origin* South and South-east Australia

15 in. *Cock:* Green, cheeks and forehead lighter. Back darker, rump deep red, under parts green shading to yellow towards the vent. Under tail coverts whitish. Wings blue-green with a yellow spot and blue edging to the flights. Beak dark horn-colour. *Hen:* Somewhat greyer in colour than the cock and lacks the red on the rump, which makes her easily recognizable.

They may be kept in an aviary with other birds, but not with their own kind. They are not finicky with their food; canary seed and millet, grass seed in the ear, fresh green food regularly and, during the breeding time, germinated seeds, form their simple menu.

Once the birds have really settled down in the flight and the nest boxes have been placed in readiness they will begin to nest. Some damp wood pulp should be placed in the box or an upturned turf pressed well into the bottom of the box answers the purpose just as well. The moisture percentage is amply sufficient; any pieces of rotten wood which are placed on top of the turf will be chewed up by the hen, and from this finely chewed substance she will shape a bowl in which she will deposit her eggs, usually 4. About 3 weeks of incubation by the hen will produce the young. During this time the cock will sit as near to the nest as

possible, and both birds will do the feeding. Once the young have left the nest for a few weeks they have to be removed and kept separately, as there is a chance that the cock will kill them when the hen starts laying a new clutch of eggs. Alternatively the cock may be housed separately for a little while.

First breeding results were reported in Britain in 1857 and in Germany in 1863. Crossings with the Rosella and the Stanley Parrakeet are on record.

A sex-linked 'yellow' mutation has been produced in England in which the green colouring of the cock is reduced to a pale yellowish-green and the red on the rump to orange. The hen of this variety is pale greyish-yellow. It is not true lutino.

### Many-coloured Parrakeet (Varied Parrakeet, Mulga Parrakeet) *Psephotus varius varius* Pl. 109

*Origin* Eastern, southern and south-western Australia

12 *in. Cock:* Upper surface mainly emerald green, tinged with blue above the eyes and on the sides of the neck; forehead, a band on the shoulders, sides and vent yellow, back of the crown, rump, abdomen and thighs crimson; throat and breast yellowish-green; flights deep greenish-blue; tail also greenish-blue, the two central feathers and bases of the remainder very dark, banded with black at the base, the outer ones tipped with pale blue; irides dark brown; beak bluish-horn with blackish tip; legs and feet dark yellowish-grey. *Hen:* Head, back, throat and breast dull greenish-grey; no yellow on the forehead or wings, the patch on the wings being dull red; abdomen and under tail coverts pale green.

The Many-coloured Parrakeet resembles the Red-rumped Parrakeet in habits and behaviour but is less hardy and when first introduced to a new aviary is inclined to be very nervous. It is especially necessary therefore to ensure that it is not frightened suddenly or it may dash wildly against the wire and seriously damage, or even kill itself. A mixture of canary seed, millet and a small quantity of oats should form its main diet together with a liberal supply of seeding grasses and green food. It nests fairly readily, using the standard type of nest box recommended for other parrakeets of the same size. The hen alone incubates, the cock feeding her at the nest, and he also assists in feeding the young. Incubation lasts about 3 weeks and when the young hatch it is advisable to supply germinating seed and a cube of brown bread dipped in milk each day, as an addition to the normal diet.

Once these birds are established it is not, as a rule, necessary to provide special conditions during the winter months but they must have a draught and frost-proof shelter in which they should be confined at night. They were first bred, by Jourdain in France, in 1877 and in England in 1902.

**Elegant Grass Parrakeet** *Neophema elegans elegans* Pl. 110

*Origin* South-western Queensland, New South Wales, Victoria and south-western Australia

9 in. *Cock:* General colour above olive-green with a golden wash; band across the forehead, extending in a narrow line over the eyes, deep blue edged with light blue on the hinder edge; lores, fore part of cheeks and throat yellow; upper breast and sides of body light golden-olive; lower breast and abdomen yellow, sometimes with an orange patch in the centre of abdomen; under tail coverts yellow; under wing coverts dark blue; tail, central feathers greenish-blue shading to blue towards the tips, remainder yellow, blue at the base; irides hazel; beak bluish-horn; legs and feet greyish-yellow. *Hen:* Duller with narrower band on forehead, less blue on wings, orange patch on abdomen absent and under tail coverts yellowish-green.

These small parrakeets are delightful aviary inhabitants but are not entirely hardy and the aviary should therefore be in a protected and sunny position and should be provided with a draught and frost-proof shelter to which they should be confined during cold nights. Their diet should consist of a mixture of two parts canary seed, two parts millet, one part oats and a very little sunflower seed, together with plenty of green food and seeding grass whenever available. Germinated seed is helpful when they are feeding young. They are said to be subject to sunstroke and although they appreciate the warmth of a sunny aviary, they should be provided with shade in the form of leafy branches or an overhanging roof. They breed well in captivity, using either nest boxes or hollow logs and incubation lasts 3 weeks. The young remain in the nest about 5 weeks and are usually extremely nervous when they first fly. Great care should therefore be taken to ensure that they are not unduly disturbed or frightened until they become thoroughly accustomed to their surroundings.

**Blue-winged Grass Parrakeet** (Blue-banded Grass Parrakeet) *Neophema chrysostomus chrysostomus*
*Origin* Victoria, South Australia, Tasmania and some Bass Strait islands.

8½ in *Cock:* Above olive-green, the head washed with yellow; lores and orbital ring yellow; a band across the forehead extending above the eyes dark ultramarine blue; cheeks, side of neck, throat and breast pale green; abdomen, flanks, thighs, under tail coverts and under side of tail yellow; wings, upper coverts bright ultramarine blue, primary coverts blackish, outer webs of some of the flights pale blue; tail, central pair of feathers blue washed with green at the base, next pair blackish with blue on the outer webs, remainder blackish, blue at the base and tipped with yellow, the yellow increasing in extent towards the outermost feathers; irides brown; beak bluish-horn, legs and feet yellowish-grey. *Hen:* Duller in colour; frontal band not so pronounced and underside greener, less yellow on abdomen.

As most of the stock now available has been bred in Britain the difficulty of acclimatization does not arise, nor are the aviary bred birds timid. They need not be kept by themselves; they agree quite well with pairs of Cockatiels, Bourke Parrakeets and such species as Virginian Cardinals and Weavers.

They are very fond of apples. Canary seed, millet, oats and hemp seed form the staple diet.

They breed well. France reported first breeding results in 1879. Crossings have been effected with the Elegant, and Turquoisine Grass Parrakeets and the Cockatiel. Their nest box should have bark on the front, below the entrance hole as they like to cling to the entrance rather than to use a perch.

**Turquoisine Grass Parrakeet** *Neophema pulchella* Pl. 103
*Origin* New South Wales, Victoria and South Australia

8 in. *Cock:* General colour above green; occiput, ear coverts and sides of neck yellowish-green; lores, line of feathers above the eyes and cheeks turquoise; broad band across the forehead deep blue; wings, upper coverts turquoise-blue, inner series chestnut-red, primary coverts and secondaries and also flights blackish-brown, dark blue on the outer webs of the former and greenish-blue on the outer webs of the flights; under coverts dark blue; tail, central feathers green, remainder green at the base of the outer webs, dark brown on inner webs and all tipped with yellow, the extent of yellow increasing towards the outermost feathers which are almost entirely yellow; throat and under surface and under tail coverts rich golden-yellow, the sides of the chest being washed with green; irides brown; beak-horn; legs and feet yellowish-grey. *Hen:* Duller generally and without chestnut-red on the wing and less blue on the face.

The Turquoisine is a bird of the twilight; it only becomes active towards the evening. It is expensive, but it breeds well.

As a rule this species begins its plans for nesting in early spring. The behaviour of the birds is then most charming to watch, and the cock sings a soft whistling song. The hen will lay 4–5 eggs in a nest containing damp moss or wood pulp, and she will incubate by herself for 17–19 days, during which time the cock will feed her on the nest. After the young are hatched the cock will continue to feed the hen for a further few days, and then they will both feed the young together. Soaked bread should be given during the rearing season, and germinated seeds; green stuff and maw seed will also be necessary.

It is wiser to purchase a pair bred in this country, for it is difficult to acclimatize newly-imported birds, even if they should be obtainable. Plenty of flying room should be available, preferably in an outside flight, where, if there is a covered-in shelter, the birds can also spend the winter.

Young birds should not be allowed to breed until they are 2 years old. This species was first bred in Germany in 1860, and has been crossed with the Elegant Grass Parrakeet.

**Splendid Grass Parrakeet** (Scarlet-chested Grass Parrakeet) *Noephema splendida* Pl. 114
*Origin* South-west Australia

Nearly 9 in. *Cock:* Head and sides of neck deep cobalt blue, remainder of upper parts green with a bluish tone on neck. Under parts are yellow with a scarlet area on the breast. Wings green with blue and black. Tail green with black and yellow. Eye brown, beak black, legs brown-black. *Hen:* Under parts olive-green, browner on upper parts. Sides of head and wings lack the blue. No scarlet on breast.

It is generally agreed that there are two different races, one with a larger area of scarlet on the crop than the other.

They are very expensive, but are undoubtedly one of the most beautiful and the best breeders of all parrakeets. Added to this they are peaceable and can be kept together with other birds. The cocks do not become aggressive even during the nesting season. Their voice is a soft whistle. They may be kept together with Bourke's Parrakeets, Cockatiels and many other species, although for breeding a pair is best kept on its own.

If a suitable aviary, facing south and well protected against the cold north and east winds, is available they may remain in this throughout the year but a good shelter should be provided, which, however, need not be heated.

Breeding results were obtained in Britain in 1872. Crossings with the Elegant and Turquoisine have been successful.

Nest boxes of 8 in. by 8 in. with a depth of 16 in. should be hung outside. Rotten wood chips or half a coconut shell should be placed inside. Successful breeding depends on correct feeding. The seed menu of canary seed, millet, hemp, oats and sunflower seed, should be augmented with apples, spinach and other green food. Incubation lasts 19 days and sometimes as many as 7 eggs will be laid. Two broods a season is no exception. The youngsters at first resemble the hen. Young cocks show odd red feathers in the crop area and a little more blue on the head.

**Bourke's Parrakeet** *Neophema bourkii* Pl. 113
*Origin* Interior of New South Wales, southern, central and western Australia

9 in. *Cock:* Above greyish-brown, darker on the rump and upper tail coverts; head and hind neck tinged with salmon-red; forehead and eyebrow stripe pale blue, the latter with white below and whitish below the eye and on front of cheeks; cheeks otherwise rosy, each feather edged brown; wings, anterior upper coverts and outer webs of flights violet-blue; tail, brownish six middle feathers tinged

with blue on the outer webs, outer feathers white with brown on the inner and blue on the outer webs at the base, under coverts pale blue; feathers of the breast brown edged with rose-pink; abdomen bright rose-pink; flanks pale blue; irides brown; beak dark horn; legs and feet brownish-grey. *Hen:* Slightly smaller, duller and paler in colour and the blue frontal band practically absent except in very old birds; head and beak also smaller.

This species is bred extensively and is therefore usually obtainable. Its soft pastel shades and beautiful dark eyes make it one of the most appealing of the Grass Parrakeets. The voice is pleasing; it sings only a few times a day and then quite softly. It will live in peace with all other small birds and will breed fairly readily.

The large dark eyes of this Parrakeet indicate that it is a bird of the twilight and really comes to life towards the evening. Like the Cockatiel, it enjoys eating the buds of such trees as apple, pear, prunus and hawthorn. Pairs become inseparable and will drink together, eat together, and roost together at night.

It is always well to find out if the birds offered for sale have just been imported or have been bred in this country, as the treatment of newly-imported birds entails much care.

They should be kept warm in the house, and should gradually become accustomed to various seeds such as canary seed, millet, oats, grass and weed seeds. Soaked seeds and rusk crumbs mixed with hard-boiled egg must be given as well. The birds should not have too much green stuff, but they need fresh branches of willow or beech. Once acclimatized they can be moved to an outside flight, but not before the end of May when sudden cold nights need no longer be feared. It is advisable to bring them indoors again when the first touch of winter comes; they should be housed in a warm room or even an unheated room. The next year they will be more hardy and can winter outside if a well-covered shelter is available.

# APPENDIX

# THE BUDGERIGAR

The Budgerigar *Melopsittacus undulatus*. Pl. 115–9
*Origin* Australia

The first live Budgerigars were brought to Europe about one hundred and thirty years ago. The normal colour is green, but yellow birds have been seen from time to time in the wild.

The Budgerigar 'came, saw and conquered', especially when it was found that it would breed freely in captivity. Opinions vary as to where the first Budgerigars were bred but the first reliable record appears to be from Germany in 1855. Although these birds were known in Great Britain as long ago as 1840, the first extensive breeding results were obtained in France and Belgium, and Holland soon became interested in these birds, so suitable as domestic pets. Belgium is the home country of the yellow Budgerigars, which, although occasionally found wild, had never before been seen in captivity. The Antwerp Zoo holds the honour of first having bred Budgerigars on a really large scale and of having given a great impetus to the keeping of these birds by fanciers.

It was after the large studs had been built up and had flourished for years (l'Etablissement Bastide at Toulouse always kept some 80,000 to 100,000 birds in stock) that the prices dropped from a very lucrative level to such low figures that breeding was barely showing a profit. Australia exported some hundreds of thousands of Budgerigars to Great Britain every year, so that today this country has such a quantity of good material that it has become possible to increase the export of good pairs to the Continent, America and other parts of the world.

To attempt to trace the beginnings of all the varieties at present extant would be too vast a subject for this book; every year sees further developments in colour and quality. Only the red Budgerigar still remains unattainable; this colour has certainly been produced now and again by artificial means; but it is not likely to become permanent unless the red factor can be introduced by crossing with some related species.

Budgerigars have been domesticated for so long that a universally recognized standard of qualities such as deportment, shape, markings and colour has been drawn up. Nowhere has the struggle to show the 'perfect' Budgerigar reached such heights as in Great Britain today. The aim is to bring the recognized colours up to the highest peak of perfection. It is regrettable that so little trouble has been taken on the Continent to get acquainted with the inherited factors, so that the beautiful deep colours could be obtained there also.

Pioneer work on the law of inheritance was carried out by Hans Steiner, Kurt Kokemüller, and Dr Duncker. The formulae worked out according to heritability of the ordinary green Budgerigar by Steiner and Duncker were respectively MMRnRnLLss and FFOObb, in which the letters denoted the various heritable factors. Ordinary people naturally fought shy of this abracadabra, and as the number of colour varieties increased, so the formulae became more and more confusing. Nevertheless, our present knowledge of colour breeding makes it unlikely that different colours will be mated together indiscriminately in future on the off-chance that some rare specimen will emerge.

As with Canaries, a methodical system is essential; one or two colours only should be chosen and raised to the peak of perfection. By this means alone can the highest awards be obtained at shows, and many people, seeing the high quality and beautiful colours of the birds, may be induced to take up the hobby of Budgerigar breeding.

Budgerigars lend themselves pre-eminently to the outdoor flight, which, if well sheltered from the north, can be their home throughout the whole year. Experience has shown that better breeding results can usually be obtained from birds kept in the open; therefore nest boxes and nesting logs should not only be hung in the shelter, but more especially in the flight. The boxes must, of course, be waterproof and hung so that heavy rain cannot penetrate to the nest and drown the young birds. If part of the flight is covered the nest boxes should be hung under the sheltering roof.

It is becoming more and more the custom to discard the old fashioned logs in favour of artificial nest boxes; the latter are roomier and offer better facilities for observation and proper control. But it would be unwise to advocate one system more than the other;

excellent results have been obtained by both. Nest boxes also have the advantage of being much cheaper and they can be easily made at home. Some breeders in Great Britain now prefer to use new nest boxes each season, and for this reason are using boxes made from thick cardboard with a wooden bottom about $1\frac{1}{2}$ in. thick, in which a shallow depression for the eggs has been chiselled out. The wooden bottoms can be obtained from the trade and fitted in any suitable box. When the breeding season is over they should be removed and the box burned. The great advantage of this is that parasites are destroyed. The bottoms should be scrubbed with a disinfectant solution. This type of box can be used equally well when breeding indoors.

All nest boxes should be provided with small ventilation holes; Budgerigars are apt to sit in the opening to the box, completely blocking it, and so preventing fresh air from reaching their young.

It would take too long to deal with all the many types of boxes on the market. The main point is that it must be possible to control the nest without disturbing the sitting birds, and without having to remove the box from the wall or cage.

Anyone should be able to choose the most suitable type for his own purpose. The best in appearance will not necessarily guarantee the production of large broods, whereas the simplest may well do so. Results really depend on the health and breeding condition of the birds themselves, rather than the type of nest provided.

It sometimes happens that a hen will, either deliberately or through carelessness, break her eggs as soon as they are laid. A useful method of saving the eggs of a hen which has developed this bad habit is to use a nest bottom with a hole in the centre of the nesting cavity, large enough for the egg to pass through. Below this hole attach a small tin filled with sawdust or other very soft material. The eggs will drop through the hole as they are laid and can then be removed and set under a more reliable hen. If a shallow glass container is used in place of the tin it is then possible to see when an egg has been laid without disturbing the nest box.

When buying a pair of Budgerigars, the date of their birth should be ascertained. Young birds should be at least 8 months old before they are allowed to breed. The hen may be a little smaller than the cock, but should not be too fat and should have a nice wide breast.

Obviously, one must expect to pay more for birds of good pedigree and colour, but it is always the wisest plan to buy young birds. After three or four years they are no longer suitable for breeding purposes, and hence there are always a great number of old birds offered on the market, but the beginner should not be tempted to buy such birds even should they be offered at a reduced price.

Cock and hen should be kept apart during the winter and the pairs should be made up early in spring. If the birds have been in cages near each other some hens may show a marked preference for certain cocks and vice versa. This natural choice is usually favourable as far as fertility is concerned, but may not always tally with the fancier's plan for special colour production. If it is desired to breed to colour, cocks and hens should be kept apart in such a way that they cannot see one another. In early spring the pairs should be placed in the breeding cages, which should be of box type with only the front of wire. In most instances the cocks and hens will accept one another, because they have no choice. Should difficulties arise, however, and the birds refuse to agree, it will be best to give the hen another husband. It may also sometimes prove advantageous to provide a cock with two hens. If at first the hens are jealous this will probably cease as soon as one hen has started to lay, and spends most of her time in the nest box. In such a case at least three nest boxes should be provided, a good distance apart.

For the production of high-class show birds, the best plan is always to breed in cages. These should be placed in a row, against a light wall and opposite windows which should be nearly always open; few birds are so dependent on light and fresh air as are budgerigars. Many of their common illnesses are caused by insufficient light or bad ventilation. Lime and cuttle fish will be eagerly taken and eaten as well as green stuff. Soaked bread and egg food may be used in addition to the normal seed mixture for the young. During the breeding period, from February onward up to laying the first egg, some cod liver oil should be dripped on to the seed and thoroughly mixed by stirring.

If it is desired to breed with Budgerigars in an outside flight and other species are to be associated with them, plenty of room is essential. Budgerigars have a trick of pulling out the nesting material from the nesting boxes occupied by other species and a bird may thus be dragged out by the tail at the same time. Serious fights with other birds rarely occur, but harmony between their own kind is not very great. Some hens may prove to be awkward and pugnacious, and the best plan is to remove them at once. A fight for a nest box occurs only when there is not sufficient choice. An extra hen in the flight will probably find a cock which will take her on as well as his own mate, but an extra cock can cause a lot of trouble. He will interfere with the mating of other birds which is not quickly performed as with other species but takes a considerable time.

It may happen that a pair of Budgerigars kept in a large cage will not begin to breed, in spite of good harmony between them. In such a case a well-mated pair can be introduced into the same cage and their good example will usually be followed.

Once breeding is on the way and eggs are being laid and incubation in progress in the various nest boxes, in no circumstances should more Budgerigars be added, for they will be persecuted and probably killed.

When a number of Budgerigars are kept together in a flight the cocks will court hens other than their own mates. The hens do not always reject these attentions and the colour breeder would be well advised not to keep varied colours together. Unexpected results can often be traced to conjugal infidelity.

Spiteful and bad natured hens do nothing except disturb nests; they often kill the young of other pairs and will even eat their own young. Such birds must be prevented from breeding, for they will never stop their bad habits.

In captivity Budgerigars will breed practically the whole year through, but late autumn and winter are, of course, not suitable times for nesting, and it is inadvisable to let a pair have more than 3 broods a year. Either the nesting facilities should be removed or the pairs separated. If the birds are outside all the winter, breeding can begin again towards the end of February, and July or August should see the beginning of the period of rest.

Suitable food for Budgerigars, in addition to various kinds of millet and canary seed, are sunflower seeds, all kinds of grass seed, young corn cobs, and green stuff such as chickweed, chicory or lettuce. Young fresh twigs, such as willow or apple branches with young buds, will also be appreciated.

The use of cuttle fish only as a means of providing calcium is undesirable; finely ground grit is also essential and extremely good for all birds, especially those that are seed eaters. They like the cuttle fish to bite on.

When breeding, as a rule the hen begins to sit after she has laid the second egg. As some clutches contain 8 eggs and the eggs are laid on alternate days, the chicks will appear at the same intervals of time. The first chick may sometimes be a fortnight older than the last to hatch, but this need cause no concern as it is quite normal. When all the young have hatched and one looks inside the nest box, they will be found neatly in a row or in a circle ranged according to age. Nests of eight are usually produced only by birds that have just begun to breed. Subsequent broods are not larger than they are in the natural state, 3 to 4 eggs. The cock feeds the hen during the 18 days of incubation. The young generally remain in the nest for about a month before they are ready to fly and by that time the hen has usually started again on a new clutch; for this she will use the same nest box and fresh eggs may be found amongst the fledglings of the first brood. The cock looks after the young after they have flown from the nest.

Birds so domesticated as Budgerigars not infrequently produce young which are deformed, with crippled legs, etc. and also an incurable baldness. This is the ultimate result of continual close inbreeding, for the young have little vitality. It is unwise to breed from old birds and they should either be disposed of or kept only as pets. Deformed young birds should be killed. The plucking of the feathers of the young, usually by the hen, is a habit which if once formed, she will never lose; the cause lies in wrong feeding – probably insufficient lime and green stuff in the diet.

Another trouble which is met with repeatedly in Budgerigars is the loss of wing and tail feathers, commonly called 'french moult', so that the birds are unable to fly. At one time this was thought to be hereditary, but today it has been attributed more to an insufficiency of oxygen during the time spent by the young birds in the nest. This is harmful to their development. When Budgerigars which have bred such young have been transferred to an outside flight they have often produced entirely healthy fledglings. Light and air must have free entry into every Budgerigar nursery.

The great expansion of the hobby of keeping Budgerigars led many fanciers to concentrate on producing as many young as possible. Hence conditions were created necessitating the regular cleaning out of nest boxes during the breeding period; this meant that the young birds had to be taken out frequently. All this is entirely unnecessary; the old birds take care that everything shall run smoothly. Of course, no lice or mite should be allowed in the boxes; if they appear, then a dusting of a suitable insecticide should be given regularly.

*Hereditability of colours*

For the creation of new life a male and female cell both possess a number of chromosomes and must unite. These cells are the gametes. When the male seed has united itself with the female egg cell, a new cell is formed which carries in itself the hereditary factors of both parents. By division of the cells only half of the original chromosomes are retained and it may be expected that with the union of the seed and the egg cell only half the hereditary factors of each parent are joined. As the chromosomes are present in the cells in pairs and are divided by reduction parting, the next union which follows will at any rate form new pairs.

Of all the factors in the chromosomes, only the colour factor is of importance to us for the moment. With a normal colour inheritance the colour chromosome of the hen united with a colour chromosome of the cock will result in a combination of both colours, but owing to the fact that certain colours are dominant and others recessive, only the dominant colour will be visible. Birds resulting from such a crossing, however, all bear in themselves the possibility of reproducing the original colour of both parents. Crossed again among themselves they will show: 25% the colour of the cock, 25% the colour of the hen, and 50% reproduce their own colour. This is according to the law of Gregor Mendel.

It is obvious, therefore, that the sex will also be tied to special chromosomes; a female of any species of bird possesses two different sex chromosomes, a male and a female, known respectively as X and Y. The male also has two chromosomes, both male, therefore XX.

With all other living creatures, except butterflies, it is exactly the opposite; the male has two different sex chromosomes and the female two similar ones.

When, with the reduction division, an X chromosome of the cock meets an X chromosome of the hen, the young bird resulting will be an XX, therefore a cock. On the other hand, if the X chromosome of the cock meets the Y chromosome of the hen, then the young bird will be XY: a hen.

If the normal colour factors are tied up to other than the sex chromosomes then everything goes according to Mendel's law, but some specific colour properties are tied to the X, therefore to the sex chromosomes, and such properties or colour mutations are inherited as sex-linked. Examples are the lutino, albino and opaline. As the Y chromosome never possesses these factors, it stands to reason that for the breeding of as many young as possible with those particular mutation factors, cocks which do possess those factors should be used for preference.

It is clear that the crossing of birds with different hereditary systems may cause chaos. When breeding, the first aim should be to form a collection of birds which, as well as being of the desired colour, should also be of as good quality as possible. It cannot be emphasized too strongly that in-breeding and incorrect selection have led to many Budgerigars being offered which in no single point meet with any of the requirements laid down by the standard.

It is regrettable that so little attention is paid to the natural type of the Budgerigar. When kept free around the house these little birds, especially the young ones, are often livelier and slimmer than they should be. Their wings are also a trifle longer.

In the colours most frequently met with nowadays, the following points should be looked for:

| | |
|---|---|
| (a) Type and Deportment. | Gracefully tapered from nape of neck to tip of tail, with an approximately straight line, and rather deep, nicely curved chest. |
| (b) Head. | Large, round, wide and symmetrical when viewed from any angle; curvature of skull commencing at cere, to rise outward and upward, continuing |

|               |                                                                                                       |
|---------------|-------------------------------------------------------------------------------------------------------|
|               | over the top and to base of head in one graceful sweep.                                               |
| (c) Eye.      | Positioned centrally, well away from front, top and back of skull.                                    |
| (d) Necklace. | Six large spots evenly spaced round throat, the size to be in keeping with the rest of the make up of the bird. |
| (e) Wings.    | Well braced and with the butts not protruding but well tucked into the sides. Flights resting just above the cushion of the tail and not crossing. |
| (f) Colour.   | Clear and level and of absolutely even shade.                                                         |
| (g) General.  | Standing at an angle of 30 degrees from the vertical, looking fearless and natural and with a completely harmonious outline. |

The basic colour is green (Light Green), with a bright yellow forehead; shoulders and wings with black markings. The grass-green colour must be absolutely even. To breed this colour to perfection, it should not be crossed with any other colour. Light Green should be mated to Light Green. Should poor fertility become apparent, then a single crossing with a Sky Blue or Opaline may be used to correct this defect.

*Dark Green* must be almost laurel in colour with black markings. In order to maintain the colour the best plan is to cross the Green with Sky Blue or Cobalt. The better the colour of the Dark Green used, the more intense will be the colour of any resulting Blues.

Therefore Dark Green/Blue × Dark Green gives a good Dark Green and Dark Green/Blue × Cobalt an excellent Cobalt.

Dark Green × Dark Green gives besides Dark Green also Light Green and Olive.

*Olive Green* mixed with deep yellow. It is difficult to breed evenly coloured birds. As a rule they will show dark patches. To maintain this colour it is best to mate Olive to Olive. Also Olive × Mauve and Olive/Blue × Olive gives a good Olive, while the Mauve will also be improved.

*Light Yellow* without markings on head and wings and with white primaries and tail. They are difficult to breed without showing a greenish tinge. Mating Light Yellow to Light Yellow is the only possible way of breeding them as pure as possible.

*Dark Yellow*, deeper yellow colour, alas generally accompanied by an even more noticeable green tinge.

*Olive Yellow*, mustard colour, without green tinge. A colour very infrequently met with.

*Sky Blue*, one of the most attractive colours. The yellow is entirely replaced by white, the green by sky blue. To maintain this colour, which should not be too pale, Sky Blues should be mated together. Should the type become poor then a single crossing with a Light Green/Blue may be made.

*Cobalt* is a darker shade than the Sky Blue and must not show any light patches. Indeed, it is even better if the colour inclines to violet. It is not correct to mate colour to colour here, although Cobalt young might be expected. It is better to mate a good Light Green/Blue bird with a Mauve one.

*Mauve* tends towards soft purple and is also extraordinarily beautiful, but the difficulty is to raise birds without cobalt patches. To maintain this colour Mauve should be mated with Olive Green/Blue.

This colour factor shows on all three of the Blues described above and if the deepest coloured bird, the violet coloured Cobalt, is taken as the ideal then a good start can be made with a cock of this colour and the same combinations used as are described for the Cobalt, in order to get the colour as deep as possible.

*White*, with either a tinge of sky blue, cobalt or mauve. White × White is the best combination, but the type suffers. In order to attain pure white, a roundabout method must be adopted, by crossing White with a Cinnamon and subsequent and continual selection of the most free of any marking. Crossing with the pure white, red-eyed Albino has little to commend it, for albino will mask any other colour.

Like the *White Wings*, which are so popular in the blue series, so are the *Yellow Wings* in the green series. To maintain this variety, colour must be mated to colour and very occasionally a White Wing × Yellow Wing.

The following are four varieties, from the many other kinds, which have now become popular:

*Albino*. Absolutely white with red eyes. It is important that size should be maintained, as they tend to become too small. Albino can mask any of the blue series; the hereditary factor of the albino is sex-linked.

*Lutino*. Butter yellow with red eyes. Also hereditary sex-linked. A single crossing with a good Light Yellow bird may benefit the type.

*Opaline*. The head and back of these birds should be entirely without markings. Seen from the back the wings are divided by a clear coloured V. Pairs should be selected with a view to eliminating all markings entirely. Hereditary sex-linked.

*Danish Pieds* is one of the most sought-after varieties. The Cinnamon Wings and the Yellow Faces are very attractive.

There are many other beautiful varieties, and many more will be bred. So much space has been devoted to Budgerigars because they enjoy such enormous popularity. Their breeding tends to become an obsession, especially because of the wide range of colours in which they can now be produced.

Many books and periodicals are published from which to extend one's knowledge. The main thing is to build one's own basic strain of birds before beginning to experiment.

The young birds will reveal the colour factors of the old birds; the pedigree of the parents is not always known but for a correct combination of colour factors this is essential. It is only after a few breeding seasons during which careful records have been kept that one can start talking of pure colours.

To make the various hereditary factors clearer a few examples are appended, in accordance with Kurt Kokemüller's table of expectations.

Green is dominant above all other colours, and blue and yellow are dominant over white.

All colours are divided into three shades, respectively light, middle and dark and the following signs, II, Id and dd can be placed before every colour to indicate the shade. In the following example II is Light Green, Id Dark Green and dd Olive.

In every colour series the following expectations apply.

|          |   | d  | d  |
|----------|---|----|----|
| II  × dd | I | Id | Id |
|          | I | Id | Id |

this means that when we take Light Green × Olive we get 100% Dark Green; similarly Sky Blue × Mauve gives 100% Cobalt.

|          |   | I  | d  |
|----------|---|----|----|
| Id  × Id | I | II | Id |
|          | d | Id | dd |

from this mating of Dark Green × Dark Green the expectation is therefore 50% Dark Green and 25% Light Green and 25% Olive.

Dark Yellow × Dark Yellow will give 25% Light Yellow, 25% Olive Yellow and 50% Dark Yellow.

|          |   | d  | d  |
|----------|---|----|----|
| Id  × dd | I | Id | Id |
|          | d | dd | dd |

therefore 50% middle colour and 50% dark, respectively Dark Green and Olive or Cobalt and Mauve.

Sex-linked hereditary may be made clear as follows: We take the cock to be XX and the hen XY.

|          |   | X  | Y  |
|----------|---|----|----|
| XX × XY  | X | XX | XY |
|          | X | XX | XY |

We now find, calculated on 100 young birds, that 50% cocks and 50% hens are born.

If we take AA to be an Albino cock and A for an Albino hen (the Y can be omitted for this cannot be an albino factor carrier) we get the following:

|         |   | A  |   |
|---------|---|----|---|
| AA × A  | A | AA | A |
|         | A | AA | A |

therefore 50% Albino cocks and 50% Albino hens.

If we now take NN for a normal cock and N for the hen, AN for the cock carrying the albino factor we get the following combinations:

| AA × N | | N | | AN × N | | N | |
|---|---|---|---|---|---|---|---|
| | A | AN | A | | A | AN | A |
| | A | AN | A | | N | NN | N |

| AN × A | | A | | NN × A | | A | |
|---|---|---|---|---|---|---|---|
| | A | AA | A | | N | AN | N |
| | N | AN | N | | N | AN | N |

For the A of Albino we can insert L for Lutino and O for Opaline or other letters for all those varieties which are sex-linked.

For the normal colour inheritance of the various non-linked colour series we can use similar diagrams by which to determine the expectations. We use letters for the various colours and remember always that cock as well as hen only give one colour chromosome each. We use capital letters for the dominant colours. G is a pure green bird (in any one of the 3 shades). G/y is a bird which is green in colour but which is the result of crossing green and yellow. G/b is a bird resulting from green and blue. GG × yy will give 100% G/y, therefore birds outwardly green but inheriting yellow thus:

| | y | y |
|---|---|---|
| G | G/y | G/y |
| G | G/y | G/y |

If G/y is now mated with G/y we get therefore (according to Mendel) 25% yellow, 25% green and 50% green inheriting yellow.

| | G | y |
|---|---|---|
| G | GG | G/y |
| y | G/y | yy |

It is, however, impossible to distinguish from outward appearances which of the 75% green coloured birds are those which carry the yellow inheriting properties.

It is interesting to note the mating of yellow and blue; all young will be green in colour but these mated among themselves produce, in addition to green, also blue, yellow and even white. Many of these green birds will pass on various colours, but they do not show which colours they can transmit and the hidden factors can only be determined by experimental matings.

This subject could be vastly extended by the use of more detailed tables, but if a beginning is made with the tables given above a stud can be started. Thereafter further research into the theory will be considerably easier.

To make it possible for everyone to check easily what may be expected from a certain mating various tables of expectations have been published. These include the colour tables of Kokemüller or a German table by Volker. A glance will show what colours may be expected, and the percentage of each.

## System of Breeding Budgerigars

The fancier who begins with a pair of very mediocre birds can hardly expect to produce therefrom a strain of prize-winners. A first-class pair, or at least one 'super' bird, should be acquired.

Not more than three broods should be taken from this pair in a season and from the resulting young the most suitable cock and hen should be selected to pair back to the old birds. If the original pair consists of a good cock and indifferent hen, then naturally only good young hens should be chosen to pair back to the old cock and the old hen should be discarded. From the second season's youngsters, the best cocks can be used. This system, which may seem a trifle unnatural, is frequently used successfully with various species of livestock.

But while in-breeding, applied with intelligence, is often successful, it will fail if thoughtless combinations are made and the wrong properties perpetuated. If the fancier feels incapable of choosing the right combinations, it is best only to mate unrelated birds. It signifies nothing that a young bird of prize-winning parents has been bought; poor fledglings are often found in the nests of prize-winners. It is advisable to look over the studs of those fanciers of good repute or to visit Shows to get some idea of what is required in a first-class bird.

There is yet another method by which a start may be made. Three pairs of the same colour series may be bought and the birds allowed to choose their own mates. It is important to see that the birds with which it is intended to begin a pedigree stud are all of even quality and suited to each other. The call of nature in such cases is difficult to understand and if two birds of indifferent types are included it is quite possible that they might mate together with unfortunate results. Birds which choose their own mates usually raise a good family. It may be assumed that the birds with which we intend to begin have been carefully chosen from good sound stock. From the results obtained during this 'free' season, much may be learned, and the different qualities shown by the youngsters will indicate the breeding quality of the parents and may form the basis on which further matings can be undertaken.

If it is found that the young from a nest have inherited only good properties from the cock and only bad properties from the hen, then the young cocks should not be mated with their mother, or these bad properties will become more apparent. The father should be mated with one of his best daughters and the best young cock with the best young sister hen.

In-breeding should be immediately discontinued when either the fertility decreases or deformed or weak youngsters are produced. The combination of half-brothers with half-sisters can be recommended as a rule, provided no similar fault is apparent in both birds.

When breeding Canaries, it is usual to replace with artificial eggs those which the hen lays, until the whole clutch is complete. A complete clutch consists of 4 eggs only with Canaries, but with Budgerigars may be as many as 8. With Budgerigars there is no sound reason to interfere with nature, so long as incubation continues. Once the young have all appeared, it may be better to transfer some to a nest containing only two or three fledglings of the same age. The numbers in the nests should, if possible, be equally divided. Thus, if one nest contains 7 young and another 3, both should be adjusted to contain 5. The Budgerigars will accept the other young without difficulty and will rear them well. The young should be ringed before moving to avoid confusion.

If the raising of Budgerigars is to be taken seriously, a simple record system is essential. The young must also be ringed to provide a means of identification. This process is best done between the 4th and 6th day after hatching. The procedure is as follows:

Take the young bird in the hand, carefully push the numbered ring over the two forward pointing toes, then over the ball of the foot and, finally, over the remaining two toes which should be pressed back against the leg. Care must be taken, however, that the ring does not pass above the elbow. Practice will make perfect. A pedigree should be kept, so as to obtain a record of the parents breeding results and also of the young birds inherited qualities.

## The Talking 'Budgie'

In addition to all the other pleasing properties of Budgerigars as pets, some, but by no means all, have an ability to repeat in a high thin voice words and even sentences.

Generally, cocks are better mimics than hens. In any case it is preferable to choose cocks for the experiment. As these birds should be taken from the breeding cage only a very few days after leaving the nest and it is then not so simple to tell cock from hen, attention should be paid to the slightest difference such as a little more blue on the nostrils, or a higher forehead.

The bird should be kept indoors, in a roomy cage, entirely out of hearing of the other birds. Now that his parents are no longer there to feed him, the young cock will probably start feeding himself, but until he does so he must be hand-fed, preferably with a dropper or a spatula.

Because Budgerigars talk with a high thin sound, they learn more readily to imitate the female voice.

The bird chosen must be absolutely tame; he must come to hand immediately and allow himself to be stroked on the back of the head. Lessons may then begin. First, a single word should be taught, e.g. he should learn his name. Then, if all goes well, a complete sentence should be repeated every time the bird is approached and so on.

Only one person should undertake the training as a frequent change of voice will only confuse the pupil. He is usually eager to learn and rapid progress can be made. A gramophone record can be used to teach him a nursery rhyme. But it must be remembered that not every Budgerigar has the same talents and some birds may prove disappointing pupils.

# INDEX OF ENGLISH NAMES

Illustration numbers are in bold figures.   The other numbers refer to text pages

# INDEX OF LATIN NAMES

Illustration numbers are in bold figures.  The other numbers refer to text pages